Y0-AQN-132

R00082 75120

CHICAGO PUBLIC LIBRARY
HAROLD WASHINGTON LIBRARY CENTER

R00082 75120

Q   Rhees, William
11   Jones, 1830-1907.
.S8
R38   An account of the
1980   Smithsonian
             Institution

DATE			

Business/Science/Technology
Division

© THE BAKER & TAYLOR CO.

AN ACCOUNT

OF

The Smithsonian Institution

This is a volume in the Arno Press collection

THREE CENTURIES
OF
SCIENCE IN AMERICA

Advisory Editor
I. Bernard Cohen

Editorial Board
Anderson Hunter Dupree
Donald H. Fleming
Brooke Hindle

See last pages of this volume for a complete list of titles

AN ACCOUNT

OF

The Smithsonian Institution

WILLIAM J. RHEES

ARNO PRESS

A New York Times Company
New York • 1980

Publisher's Note: This book has been reproduced from the best available copy.

Editorial supervision: Steve Bedney

———————

Reprint Edition 1980 by Arno Press Inc.

Reprinted from a copy in the University of Illinois Library

THREE CENTURIES OF SCIENCE IN AMERICA
ISBN for complete set: 0-405-12525-9
See last pages of this volume for titles.

Manufactured in the United States of America

———————

Library of Congress Cataloging in Publication Data

Rhees, William Jones, 1830-1907.
 An account of the Smithsonian Institution.

 (Three centuries of science in America)
 Reprint of the 1859 ed. published by T. McGill,
Washington.
 1. Smithsonian Institution. I. Title.
II. Series.
Q11.S8R38 1980   069'.09753   79-8404
ISBN 0-405-12582-8

SST
Cop. 2

AN ACCOUNT

OF

The Smithsonian Institution

W WADE DEL.   J.RENWICK JR. ARCHITECT   W ROBERTS SC

AN ACCOUNT

OF

𝕿𝖍𝖊 𝕾𝖒𝖎𝖙𝖍𝖘𝖔𝖓𝖎𝖆𝖓 𝕴𝖓𝖘𝖙𝖎𝖙𝖚𝖙𝖎𝖔𝖓,

ITS

FOUNDER, BUILDING, OPERATIONS, ETC.,

PREPARED FROM THE

ιEPORTS OF PROF. HENRY TO THE REGENTS, AND OTHER AUTHENTIC SOURCES.

BY WILLIAM J. RHEES.

WASHINGTON:
THOMAS McGILL, PRINTER.

OFFICERS OF THE SMITHSONIAN INSTITUTION.

JAMES BUCHANAN, *Ex-Officio* Presiding Officer of the Institution.
ROGER B. TANEY, Chancellor of the Institution.
JOSEPH HENRY, Secretary of the Institution.
SPENCER F. BAIRD, Assistant Secretary.
W. W. SEATON, Treasurer.
WILLIAM J. RHEES, Chief Clerk.
ALEXANDER D. BACHE, ⎫
JAMES A. PEARCE, ⎬ Executive Committee.
JOSEPH G. TOTTEN, ⎭

REGENTS OF THE INSTITUTION.

JOHN C. BRECKENRIDGE	Vice President of the United States.
ROGER B. TANEY	Chief Justice of the United States.
JAMES G. BERRET	Mayor of the City of Washington.
JAMES A. PEARCE	Member of the United States Senate.
JAMES M. MASON	Member of the United States Senate.
STEPHEN A. DOUGLAS	Member of the United States Senate.
WM. H. ENGLISH	Member of the House of Representatives.
L. J. GARTRELL	Member of the House of Representatives.
BENJAMIN STANTON	Member of the House of Representatives.
GIDEON HAWLEY	Citizen of New York.
RICHARD RUSH	Citizen of Pennsylvania.
GEORGE E. BADGER	Citizen of North Carolina.
CORNELIUS C. FELTON	Citizen of Massachusetts.
ALEXANDER D. BACHE	Citizen of Washington.
JOSEPH G. TOTTEN	Citizen of Washington.

MEMBERS EX-OFFICIO OF THE INSTITUTION.

JAMES BUCHANAN	President of the United States.
JOHN C. BRECKENRIDGE	Vice President of the United States.
LEWIS CASS	Secretary of State.
HOWELL COBB	Secretary of the Treasury.
JOHN B. FLOYD	Secretary of War.
ISAAC TOUCEY	Secretary of the Navy.
JOSEPH HOLT	Postmaster General.
JEREMIAH S. BLACK	Attorney General.
ROGER B. TANEY	Chief Justice of the United States.
W. D. BISHOP	Commissioner of Patents.
JAMES G. BERRET	Mayor of the City of Washington.

HONORARY MEMBERS.

ROBERT HARE*	Pennsylvania.
WASHINGTON IRVING	New York.
BENJAMIN SILLIMAN	Connecticut.
PARKER CLEAVELAND*	Maine.
A. B. LONGSTREET	Mississippi.
JACOB THOMPSON	Secretary of the Interior.

* Deceased.

Entered according to Act of Congress, in the year 1859, by WILLIAM J. RHEES, in the Clerk's Office of the District Court for the District of Columbia.

INTRODUCTION.

The Smithsonian Institution has attained a world-wide reputation, and its influence and importance are constantly extending. Its publications are found not only in the public libraries of our own land, but also in those of every other civilized country. Its correspondents include some of the most distinguished cultivators of science of the present day, and it is referred to as a center of information by those who are interested in the pursuit of knowledge.

Many persons, however, who visit Washington, are but imperfectly acquainted with the history of Smithson, the great object he had in view, the plans adopted to carry out his intentions, and the results already obtained. It is for the purpose of furnishing more definite information on these points that this work has been compiled, from the annual reports of the Secretary, Professor HENRY, to the Board of Regents, and other authentic sources.

THE SMITHSONIAN INSTITUTION.

The Founder.

JAMES SMITHSON, the founder of the Institution which bears his name and will perpetuate his memory, was a native of London, England. In his will he states that he was the son of Hugh, first Duke of Northumberland, and Elizabeth, heiress of the Hungerfords, of Audley, and niece of Charles the Proud, Duke of Somerset. He was educated at Oxford, where he took an honorary degree in 1786. He went under the name of James Lewis Macie until a few years after he had left the university, when he took that of Smithson, the family name of the Northumberlands. He does not appear to have had any fixed home in England, but travelled much on the continent, occasionally staying a year or two in Paris, Berlin, Florence, etc. He died at Genoa, in 1828, at an advanced age. He is said by Sir Davies Gilbert, President of the Royal Society, to have rivalled the most expert chemists in minute analysis; and, as an instance of his skill, it is mentioned that, happening to observe a tear gliding down a lady's cheek, he endeavored to catch it on a crystal vessel; that half of the drop escaped, but having preserved the other half, he submitted it to close analysis, and discovered in it several salts. He contributed a number of valuable papers to the Royal Society, and also to the Annals of Philosophy, on chemistry, mineralogy, and geology. His scientific reputation was founded on these branches, though from his writings he appears to have studied and reflected upon almost every department of knowledge. He was of a sensitive, retiring disposition; was never married—appeared ambitious of making a name for himself.

either by his own researches or by founding an institution for the promotion of science. He declared, in writing, that though the best blood of England flowed in his veins, this availed him not, for his name would live in the memory of man when the titles of the Northumberlands and Percies were extinct or forgotten. He was cosmopolitan in his views, and affirmed that the man of science is of no country—the world is his country, and all men his countrymen. He proposed at one time to leave his money to the Royal Society of London, for the promotion of science, but on account of a misunderstanding with the council of the Society he changed his mind, and left it to his nephew, and in case of the death of this relative, to the United States of America, to found the Institution which now bears his name.

The Bequest.

The whole amount of money received from the bequest was $515,169; and, besides this, $25,000 was left in England as the principal of an annuity to the mother of the nephew of Smithson. This sum will also come to the Institution. The Government of the United States accepted the bequest, or in other words, accepted the office of trustee, and the Hon. Richard Rush, of Pennsylvania, was charged with the duty of prosecuting the claim. He remained in attendance on the English courts until the money was awarded to him. He brought it over in sovereigns, deposited it in the Mint of the United States, where it was recoined into American eagles, thus becoming a part of the currency of the country.

At the time of the passing of the act establishing the Institution, in 1846, the sum of $242,000 had accrued in interest, and this the Regents were authorized to expend on a building. But, instead of appropriating this sum immediately to this purpose, they put it at interest, and deferred the completion of the building for several years, until over $100,000 should be accumulated, the income of which might defray the expenses of keeping the building, and the greater portion of the income of the original bequest be devoted to the objects for which it was designed. This policy has been rigidly adhered to, and the result is, that, besides the original sum, and after all that has been devoted to the building, the grounds, and other operations, there is now on hand, of accumulated interest, $125,000, which has been invested in State stocks.

The Plan of Organization.

The bequest, in the language of the testator, was "to found at Washington an establishment, under the name of the Smithsonian Institution, for the increase and diffusion of knowledge among men." According to this, the Government of the United States is merely a trustee. The bequest is *for the benefit of mankind*, and any plan which does not recognize this provision of the will would be illiberal and unjust. The Institution must bear and perpetuate the name of its founder, and hence its operations are kept distinct from those of the General Government, and all the good which results from the expenditure of the funds is accredited to the name of Smithson.

It will be observed that the object of the bequest is twofold—first, to *increase*, and, second, to *diffuse*, knowledge among men. These two objects are entirely separate and distinct, and to view the case understandingly the one must not be confounded with the other. The first is to enlarge the existing stock of knowledge by the addition of new truths, and the second, to disseminate knowledge thus enlarged among men. This distinction is readily acknowledged by men of science, and in Europe different classes of scientific and other societies are founded upon it. The will makes no restriction in favor of any particular kind of knowledge, and hence all branches are entitled to a share of attention. Smithson was well aware that knowledge should not be viewed as existing in isolated parts, but as a whole, each portion of which throws light on all the others, and that the tendency of all is to improve the human mind, and to give it new sources of power and enjoyment. A prevalent idea, however, in relation to the will is, that the money was intended exclusively for the diffusion of *useful* or immediately practical knowledge among the inhabitants of this country, but it contains nothing from which such an inference can be drawn. All knowledge is useful, and the higher the more important. From the enunciation of a single scientific truth may flow a hundred inventions, and the more abstract the truth the more important the deductions. To effect the greatest good, the organization of the Institution should be such as to produce results which could not be attained by other means, and inasmuch as the bequest is for men in general, all merely local expenditures are inconsistent with the will. These were the views expressed by the Secretary, Professor Henry, and constantly advocated by him. They were not entertained, however, by many, and consequently difficulties have been encountered in carrying them out. A number of literary men thought that a great *library* should be founded at Washington, and all the money expended on it; others considered a *museum* the proper object; and another class thought the income should be devoted to the delivery of *lectures* throughout the country; while still another was of opinion that popular *tracts* should be published and distributed amongst the million. But all these views were advanced without a proper examination of the will, or a due consideration of the smallness of the income. The act of Congress directed the formation of a library, a museum, a gallery of art, lectures, and a building on a liberal scale to accommodate these objects. One clause, however, gave the Regents the power, after the foregoing objects were provided for, to expend the remainder of the income in any way they might think fit for carrying out the design of the testator. The plan they have adopted is to stimulate all persons in this country capable of advancing knowledge by original research to labor in this line; to induce them to send their results to the Institution for examination and publication; and to assist all persons engaged in original investigations, as far as its means will allow; also to institute, at the expense and under the direction of the Institution, particular researches. This plan has been found eminently practicable, and by means of it the Institution has been enabled to produce results which have made it favorably known in every part of the civilized world.

What has been done.

As an evidence of the above assertion, the following facts are given in a late report of the Regents to Congress :

" The Institution has promoted *astronomy*, by the aid furnished the researches which led to the discovery of the true orbit of the new planet Neptune, and the determination of the perturbations of this planet, and the other bodies of the solar system, on account of their mutual attraction. It has also aided the same branch of science by furnishing instruments and other facilities to the Chilian Expedition, under Lieutenant Gilliss, and by preparing and publishing an ephemeris of Neptune, which has been adopted by all the astronomers of the world. It has also published maps, and instructions for the observation of eclipses. It has advanced *geography*, by providing the scientific traveler with the annual lists of occultations of the principal stars by the moon, for the determination of longitude; by the preparation of tables for ascertaining heights with the barometer; and by the collection and publication of important facts relative to the topography of different parts of the country, particularly of the Valley of the Mississippi. It has established an extended system of *meteorology*, consisting of a corps of several hundred intelligent observers, who are daily noting the phases of the weather in every part of the continent of North America. It has imported standard instruments, constructed hundreds of compared thermometers, barometers, and psychrometers, and has furnished improved tables and directions for observing, with their instruments, the various changes of the atmosphere, as to temperature, pressure, moisture, etc. It has collected, and is collecting, from its observers, an extended series of facts, which are yielding deductions of great interest in regard to the climate of this country, and the meteorology of the globe.

" The Institution has advanced the science of *geology*, by its researches and original publications. It has made a preliminary exploration of the remarkable region of the Upper Missouri River called the " Bad Lands," and has published a descriptive memoir on the extraordinary remains which abound in that locality. It has assisted in explorations relative to the distribution in this country of the remains of microscopic animals found in immense quantities in different parts of the United States. It has made important contributions to *botany*, by means of the published results of explorations in Texas, New Mexico, and California, and by the preparation and publication of an extended memoir, illustrated with colored engravings, on the sea-plants of the coast of North America. It has published several important original papers on *physiology, comparative anatomy, zoology*, and different branches of descriptive *natural history ;* and has prepared and printed, for distribution to travelers and others, a series of directions for collecting and preserving specimens. It has advanced *terrestrial magnetism*, by furnishing instruments for determining the elements of the magnetic force, to various exploring expeditions, and by publishing the results of observations made under its direction at the expense of the Government.

" The Institution has also been instrumental in directing attention to American *antiquities*, and has awakened such an interest in the subject as will tend to the collection of all the facts which can be gathered relative to the ancient inhabitants of this continent. It has also rendered available, for the purposes of the ethnologist and philanthropist, the labors of our missionaries among the Dacotahs, by publishing a volume on the language of this tribe of Indians; and has done good service to comparative *philology*, by the distribution of directions for collecting Indian vocabularies.

" It has established an extended system of literary and scientific *exchanges*, both foreign and domestic, and annually transmits between the most distant societies and individuals thousands of packages of valuable works. It has presented its own publications, free of expense, to all the first class libraries in the world, thus rendering them accessible, as far as possible, to all persons who are interested in their study. No restriction of copyright has been placed on their republication, and the truths which they contain are daily finding their way to the general public through the labor of popular writers and teachers. The distribution of its publications, and its system of exchanges, has served not only to advance and diffuse knowledge, but also to increase the reputation, and consequently the influence, of our country—to promote a kindly and sympathetic feeling between the New World and the Old, alike grateful to the philosopher and the philanthropist.

" These are the fruits of what is called, the system of active operations of the Institution; and its power to produce other and continuous results is only limited by the amount of the income which can be appropriated to it, since each succeeding year has presented new and important fields for its cultivation. All the anticipations with regard to it have been more than realized."

The following extract from a speech delivered in the House of Representatives, February 27, 1855, by one of the Regents, Hon. William H. English, of Indiana, gives an excellent and comprehensive view of the condition of the Institution:

* * * " Look at the financial department, where corruption would most likely exist, if it existed at all, and you will find the gratifying fact that it has been so judiciously managed, that, after paying all the current expenses, the funds and property are this day worth double the amount of the original bequest. Where, sir, in this age of extravagant expenditures of public money and deficiency bills will you find a parallel to this? The Regents are authorized to expend all the accruing interest; but so far from doing so, they have, by husbanding their resources, and by constant watchfulness over the disbursements, actually saved the sum of $125,000, which they have now on hand to apply as a permanent addition to the principal. What, then, is the result? A magnificent building, of ample dimensions, has been erected, at a cost of $300,000. Books, apparatus, and other articles have been provided for the library, museum, laboratory, and gallery of art, worth $85,000. Lecturers have been employed, original researches have

been made, many valuable and scientific works published and distributed, the current expenses entirely paid, and yet the principal is increased $125,000. And of the interest expended, I have yet to hear where one dollar was devoted to an improper purpose. Does this look as if the Institution was badly managed? If I am asked what the Institution has done to carry out the object for which it was designed, I reply that it has already done much although yet in its infancy. The building is just completed, and it is not to be expected that a great establishment, which is to exist as long as this Government itself, is to be built up in a day. The foundation is being laid deep and wide, and the noble work is gradually but surely advancing."

The Government.

An act of Congress, dated August 10, 1846, provides " that the President and Vice-President of the United States, the Secretary of State, the Secretary of the Treasury, the Secretary of War, the Secretary of the Navy, the Postmaster General, the Attorney General, the Chief Justice, and the Commissioner of the Patent Office of the United States, and the Mayor of the City of Washington, during the time for which they shall hold their respective offices, and such other persons as they may elect as honorary members, be and they are hereby constituted an ' establishment,' by the name of the ' Smithsonian Institution,'' for the increase and diffusion of knowledge among men."

The law also provides for a " Board of Regents," to be composed of the Vice-President of the United States and the Mayor of the City of Washington, during the time for which they shall hold their respective offices, three members of the Senate and three members of the House of Representatives, together with six other persons, other than members of Congress, two of whom shall be members of the National Institute, in the City of Washington, and resident in the said city; and the other four shall be inhabitants of other States, and no two of them from the same State.

The Establishment exercises general supervision over the affairs of the Institution.

The Board of Regents conducts the business of the Institution, and makes annual reports to Congress.

The Secretary of the Institution is elected by the Board. His duty is to take charge of the building and property, discharge the duty of librarian, keeper of the museum, etc., and has power, by consent of the Regents, to employ assistants.

All laws for the protection of public property in Washington apply to the lands, buildings, and other property of the Institution.

The Structure.

The Smithsonian building stands on a part of a tract of public land denom. inated "the Mall," and the grounds extend from Seventh to Twelfth streets, east and west, and from the canal to B street, north and south, comprising about fifty-two acres. The center of the building is directly opposite Tenth street, and the site is about twenty feet above the average level of Pennsylvania avenue.

The style of architecture is that of the last half of the twelfth century, the latest variety of the rounded style, as it is found immediately anterior to its merging into the early Gothic, and is known as the Norman, the Lombard, or Romanesque. The semi-circular arch, stilted, is employed throughout—in doors, windows, and other openings.

It is the first edifice in the style of the twelfth century, and of a character not ecclesiastical, ever erected in this country.

The main building has in the center of its north front two towers, of which the higher reaches an elevation of about 150 feet. On the south front is a massive tower 37 feet square and 91 feet high. On the northeast corner stands a double companile tower, 17 feet square and 117 feet high; at the southwest corner an octagonal tower, in which is a spiral stair case. There are nine towers in all.

NORTH CENTRAL TOWERS.

The entire length of the building, from east to west, is 447 feet. Its greatest breadth is 160 feet. The east wing is 82 by 52 feet, and 42½ feet high to the top of its battlement; the west wing, including its projecting apsis, is 84 feet by 40, and 38 feet high, and each of the connecting ranges, including its cloister, is 60 feet by 49 The main building is 205 feet by 57, and, to the top of the corbel course, 58 feet high.

The building is erected in a very substantial manner. The foundation walls under the main central towers are 12 feet thick at bottom, gradually diminishing to five feet six inches at the surface of the ground, and are sunk eight feet deep. The thickness of the walls of the main building above the water table is two feet and-a-half in the first story, and two feet in the second, exclusive of buttresses, corbel courses, &c. The walls of the wings are two feet thick; of the central towers three feet and a half thick in the first story, diminishing to two feet in the highest story. The roofs are slated. The face of the building is finished in ashlar, laid in courses from 10 to 15 inches in height, and having an average bed of nine inches.

The material employed is a lilac gray variety of freestone, found in the new red sandstone formation where it crosses the Potomac, near the mouth of Seneca Creek, one of its tributaries, and about twenty-three miles above Washington. When first quarried it is comparatively soft, working freely before the chisel and hammer; but by exposure it gradually indurates, and ultimately acquires tough-ness and consistency, that not only enables it to resist the changes of the atmos-phere, but even the most severe mechanical wear and tear.

The corner-stone of the building was laid with Masonic ceremonies, on the first of May, 1847, in the presence of President Polk, his Cabinet, and an immense concourse of citizens and strangers. The Grand Master of Masons, who performed the ceremony, wore the apron presented by the Grand Lodge of France to Wash-ington, through La Fayette, and used the gavel employed by Washington when he laid the first corner-stone of the Capitol of the United States. An oration was delivered by the Hon. George Mifflin Dallas, the first Chancellor of the Smithsonian Institution, and now United States Minister to Great Britain. In the course of his remarks Mr. Dallas said : " When, at no distant day, I trust, it shall be seen that within the walls of this building the truths of nature are forced by persever_ ing researches from their hidden recesses, mingled with the stock already hoarded by genius and industry, and thence profusely scattered, by gratuitous lectures or publications, for the benefit of all—when it shall be seen that here universal science finds food, implements, and a tribune—art her spring to invention, her studio, and her models ; and both shall have throngs of disciples from the ranks of our people, emulous for enlightenment, or eager to assist—then the condition of our legacy will have been performed, and the wide philanthropy of Smithson have achieved its aim."

The design, by James Renwick, Jr., of New York, consists of a main center building, two stories high, and two wings, connected by intervening ranges; each of these latter having, on the north or principal front, a cloister, with open stone screen.

The first story of the main building consists of one large room, 200 feet by 50, and 25 feet high, the ceiling of which is supported by two rows of columns ex-tending the whole length ; at the middle of the space corresponding to the prin-cipal entrances are two wing walls, by which, with the addition of screens, the whole space may be divided into two large rooms, with a hall extending across the

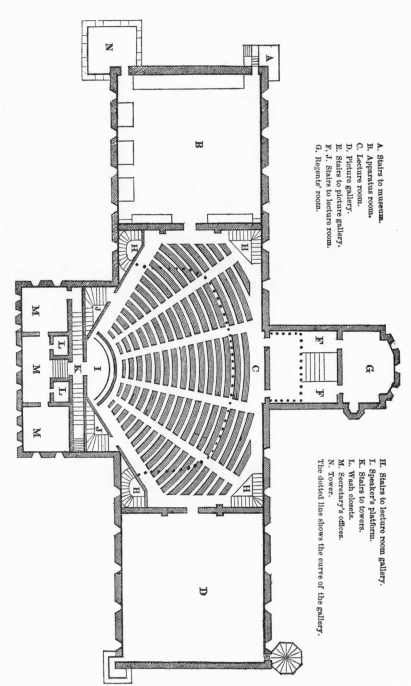

A. Stairs to museum.
B. Apparatus room.
C. Lecture room.
D. Picture gallery.
E. Stairs to picture gallery.
F, J. Stairs to lecture room.
G. Regents' room.

H. Stairs to lecture room gallery.
I. Speaker's platform.
K. Stairs to towers.
L. Wash closets.
M. Secretary's offices.
N. Tower.
The dotted line shows the curve of the gallery.

GROUND PLAN OF THE SECOND FLOOR.

THE LECTURE ROOM.

building between them. This story may be used for a library or a museum, or
for both, as the wants of the Institution may require. It is finished in a simple
but chaste style, and has received general commendation. It is one of the most
imposing rooms in this country, apart even from adaptation to its purposes.

The upper story is divided into three apartments without pillars—a lecture-
room in the middle, and two rooms, each 50 feet square, on either side. The
one on the east is for apparatus, and for meetings of societies, committees, &c. ;
that on the west is now occupied by Stanley's Indian Gallery and other collections.

The whole arrangement of the upper part of the building is made with a view
to afford facilities for meetings of associations, which have for their object the
promotion, diffusion or application of knowledge. If at any time the space
now occupied by the lecture-room should be required for other purposes, the seats
and gallery may be removed, and the partition walls, which are unconnected with
the roof, may be taken down, and the whole upper story converted into a large hall.

The Lecture Room.

The optic and acoustic properties of the lecture-room are unsurpassed by any
apartment, intended for the same purpose, in the United States. As has been
observed, it is situated in the second story of the main building; it is one hundred feet in length, and, by occupying part of the towers, a width of seventy-five
feet has been secured. The ceiling is twenty-five feet high, smooth and unbroken,

with the exception of an oval opening above to admit light on the platform. It thus powerfully reflects the sound of the speaker's voice to the hearers, and being so low, this reflection blends with the original sound and simply re-enforces it.

The general form of the room is fan-shaped, the speaker being near the handle of the fan, on one side of the room. The walls behind and near him are smooth lath and plaster, giving a powerful but short resonance, which strengthens his voice. Not being parallel, they reduce the reverberation, but send the sound out from the speaker, to increase the volume of his voice until it reaches the furthest part of the gallery. The multitude of surfaces directly in front of the speaker—gallery, pillars, stair-screens, and the seats of the audience—prevent reverberation. The seats are curved, so that each spectator faces the platform; and the floor is also curved, so that the back seats rise above the front—not quite so much as is required by the *panoptic* curve of Professor Bache, but as much as the size of the room will allow. The gallery is in the form of a horse-shoe. The architecture of this room is due to Captain Alexander, of the corps of Topographical Engineers, who varied the plan until the required conditions were, as nearly as possible, fulfilled. The room will seat fifteen hundred persons, and when crowded will contain upwards of two thousand. Prof. Henry presented a valuable paper on acoustics to the American Association for the Advancement of Science, at its meeting in Albany, August, 1856. It gives an account of the principles on which the Smithsonian lecture-room was constructed, and the result of the observations made by Capt. Meigs, Prof. Bache, and Prof. Henry, in relation to the new rooms in the extension of the Capitol. It was published in the transactions of the Association, and in the Smithsonian Report for 1856.

REGENTS' ROOM.

The room in the second story of the south tower is used for the meetings of the Board of Regents. The offices of the Secretary are in the north tower, immediately in front of the lecture room; the library is at the west end; the natural history department, chemical laboratory, exchange, and publication rooms, at the east end of the building.

Regents' Room.

In the room used by the "Regents" and the "Establishment" as a hall for their meetings, are now deposited the personal effects of James Smithson. Here may be seen his trunks, umbrella, walking-cane, sword, plume, riding-whip, a set of silver plate, a miniature chemical laboratory which he used when travelling, thermometers, snuff box, scales, candlesticks, &c.

Hanging in this room is an original painting by Bergham, a rural scene, the property of Smithson, a marble head of St. Cecilia, by Thorwalsden, &c.

There are also likenesses of Chief Justice Taney, Chancellor of the Institution, Hon. Richard Rush, of Pennsylvania, and Senator Pearce, of Maryland, distinguished alike for their devotion to the interests of the Institution, of which they have been Regents from its organization, and for their valuable public services.

The Library.

This portion of the establishment has been well filled by purchase, donation, the copyright law, and exchange. It now contains 25,000 very valuable volumes, and is rapidly becoming of much value in its special sphere of usefulness. In relation to it, the Secretary, in his report for 1855, says:

"It is the present intention of the Regents to render the Smithsonian Library the most extensive and perfect collection of transactions and scientific works in this country, and this it will be enabled to accomplish by means of its exchanges, which will furnish it with all the current journals and publications of societies, while the separate series may be completed in due time as opportunity and means may offer. The Institution has already more complete sets of transactions of learned societies than are to be found in the oldest libraries in the United States, and on this point we speak on the authority of one of the first bibliographers of the day. This plan is in strict accordance with the general policy of the Institution, viz: to spend its funds on objects which cannot as well be accomplished by other means, and has commended itself to those who are able to appreciate its merits, and who are acquainted with the multiplicity of demands made upon the limited income of the Smithsonian fund. In a letter, after a visit to Washington, the bibliographer before alluded to remarks: 'My previous opinions as to the judiciousness of the system pursued by the Smithsonian Institution, in every respect, were more than confirmed. I hope you will not change in the least. Your exchanges will give you the most important of all the modern scientific publications, and the older ones can be added as you find them necessary. The Library, I think, should be confined strictly to works of science.'"

Besides books, the Library contains engravings, maps, music, and other articles connected with the art of printing. The collection of engravings and works upon

THE LIBRARY.

the history of art is believed to be one of the choicest in the country. It was made by an American gentleman distinguished as a scholar no less than as a statesman, with a special design of illustrating the process and resources of the art of engraving, in all its branches, from its early masters to its present time. This collection contains some of the best works of nearly every engraver of much celebrity. There is one portfolio of the works of Albert Durer, containing twenty engravings on copper and two on iron by his own hand—and among them most of his best and rarest works; about sixty fine copies on copper, including the famous seventeen by Marc Antonio; thirteen different portraits of Durer, and a large number of wood cuts engraved by him or under his inspection. Another port. folio contains a large collection of the etchings of Rembrandt, including some of his most beautiful pieces, particulary the "Christ Healing the Sick," an early and fine impression. There is a portfolio of two hundred engravings and etchings, by Claude Lorraine, Hollar, and Bega; a portfolio of superb portraits by Nanteuil, Wille, Edelink, and others, among them a first impression of the "Louis XIV in

2

armor," by Nanteuil; a portfolio of prints from the old Italian masters, comprising many that are extremely rare; and another from the old German masters, containing about one hundred prints, many of them scarce and of great beauty. There are, besides, five portfolios of sheet engravings, including very choice prints. Among them are thirty-one which are valued by Longhi at fifteen hundred dollars.

Among the galleries and published collections, are the "Musée Royal," in two volumes folio, proofs before the letter, a superb copy; Denon's "Monumens des Arts du Dessin," in four volumes folio, of which only two hundred and fifty copies were published; Baillie's Works, one hundred plates, folio; Thorwaldsen's Works, four volumes, folio; Hogarth's Works, folio, and the German edition in quarto; The Boydell Gallery, two volumes, folio; Boydell's "Shakspeare Gallery," a remarkably good copy, containing many proofs before the letter, numerous etchings and several progressive plates; Claude's "Liber Veritatis," an original copy, three volumes, folio; The Houghton Gallery, two volumes, folio; Chamberlain's Drawings in the Royal Collection, one volume, folio; Rembrandt's Drawings, one volume, quarto; Da Vinci's Drawings, one volume, quarto; "Galerie de Florence;" Angerstein Gallery; Ancient Sculpture, by the Dilettanti Society; Perrault's "Hommes Illustres;" Sadeler's Hermits; "Theuerdank," a fine copy of the very rare edition of 1519; Meyrick's Armor; Hope's Ancient Costumes, and more than one hundred volumes besides, mostly in folio or quarto, either composed entirely of valuable engravings, or in which the text is published for the sake of the illustrations of fine or decorative art.

The collection of critical and historical works, in the various departments of the fine arts, comprises several hundred volumes of the best works in the English, French, German, and Italian languages, including whatever is mostly needed by the student of art in all its branches.

The Library is open to the public from 9 a. m. to 5 p. m. daily, except Sunday.

The busts in the Library represent the Hon. Roger B. Taney, Chief Justice of the United States and Chancellor of the Institution; Robert Fulton, Commodore Decatur, Joel Barlow, Thomas Jefferson, Daniel Webster, Milton, Thorwalsden, and Benjamin Hallowell.

The Reading Room.

The visitor will find in the Reading-room, which adjoins the Library, the leading periodicals, and particularly the scientific journals published in the world.

In this room may be seen a portrait of Smithson, representing him in the costume of a student of Oxford, which was probably painted when he was not more than twenty years of age. This portrait was purchased for thirty guineas, for the Institution, by the Hon. Abbot Lawrence, from the widow of John Fitall, a servant of Smithson mentioned in his will. There is also in possession of the Institution a medallion of Smithson, in copper, taken in after life.

On the west porch, adjoining the Reading-room, are several idols from Central America, presented to the Institution by E. G. Squier, late United States Minis-

THE READING ROOM.

ter to Nicaragua. The largest statue, carved in black basalt, was obtained from the Island of Momotombita, in Lake Managua, where there was a temple or sacred place. The figure with the sphinx-like head-dress is also from the same locality. One or two of the other statues, by the Indians of the Pueblo of Subtiava, near Leon, having been buried a great number of years, and the locality carefully concealed, they are somewhat mutilated. A small group of these monuments exists in the depths of the forest midway between Leon and the Pacific, which is still secretly visited by the Indians for the performance of dances and other rites pertaining to their primitive religion. The small figure resembling some animal *couchant* was, until very recently, preserved on a remarkable rock on the side of the volcano of Omatepec, and regarded with high veneration by the Indians. It was only after many years of search that the priests were able to find and remove it. The granite vase, distinguished by the ornaments called *grecques* by Humboldt, (and which characterize the ruins at Mitla, in Mexico,) was dug up near the city of Nicaragua. The spot had been a cemetery of the ancient inhabitants.

Another relic of the same material, and with a like style of ornament, accompanies the vase, and was found in the same neighborhood. It seems to have been designed as a pedestal for a small statue. There are also several vases, in which the bones and ashes of the dead were packed after the decomposition of the flesh or after burning.

The largest and most elaborate monuments in Nicaragua exist in the little Island of Pensacola, near the base of the extinct volcano of Momobacho. They weigh a number of tons each, and are distinguished as being wrought from blocks of sandstone—a material which is not found on the island. Two of the statues of the Smithsonian collection are from the Island of Zapatero, in Lake Nicaragua, where once existed one of the most imposing aboriginal temples of the country. Here, among the ruins of the *teocalli*, or high-places of the former inhabitants, were found entire statues, besides the fragments of many others, several broken sacrificial stones, etc.

The Museum.

The Smithsonian Institution is now in possession of the best collection of the larger North American and European mammalia, both skins and skeletons, to be found in the United States. In birds it is only second to the collection of the Philadelphia Academy of Natural Sciences—the latter being without doubt the most extensive and perfect now extant. Of fish the Smithsonian has a greater number than is to be found in any cabinet, except that of Professor Agassiz.

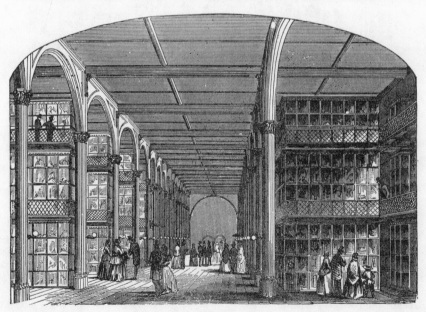

THE MUSEUM.

LABORATORY OF NATURAL HISTORY

It should be understood that the Smithsonian Institution does not enter upon grounds already occupied, and therefore it is not an object to collect specimens promiscuously, or those usually found in other museums.   Hence the collection of this Institution is not attractive to the general visitor and curiosity seeker; but the student of natural history will here find much that will be sought in vain else-where.   Duplicate specimens are often exchanged for those in other collections, and all the objects are open for the study and examination of those engaged in this line of research.   Applications for such facilities are numerous, and have al-ways been granted.   The preparation of most of the important papers on natural history published within a few years in this country has been aided in this way by the Institution.

The act of Congress establishing the Institution provides as follows :—

Sec. 6. That, in proportion as suitable arrangements can be made for their reception, all objects of art and of foreign and curious research, and all objects of natural history, plants, and geological and mineralogical specimens belonging, or hereafter to belong, to the United States, which may be in the city of Washington, in whosesoever custody the same may be, shall be delivered to such persons as may be authorized by the Board of Regents to receive them, and shall be arranged in such order, and so classed, as best facilitate the exam-ination and study of them, in the building so as aforesaid to be erected for the Institution ; and the Regents of said Institution shall afterwards, as new specimens in natural history, geology, or minerology, may be obtained for the museum of the Institution, by exchange of duplicate specimens belonging to the Institution, (which they are hereby authorized to make,) or by any donation, which they may receive, or otherwise, cause such new specimens to be also appropriately classed and arranged.

Under these provisions, the Institution has received and taken charge of such government collections in mineralogy, geology, and natural history as have been made since its organization.   The amount of these has been very great, as all the United States Geological, Boundary and Railroad Surveys, with the various topographical, military, and naval explorations, have been, to a greater or less extent, ordered to make such collections as would illustrate the physical and natural history features of the regions traversed.

Of the collections made by thirty government expeditions, those of twenty-five are now deposited with the Smithsonian Institution, embracing more than five-sixths of the whole amount of materials collected.   The principal expeditions thus furnishing collections are the United States Geological Surveys of Doctors Owen, Jackson, and Evans, and of Messrs. Foster and Whitney ; the United States and Mexican Boundary Survey ; the Pacific Railroad Survey ; the Exploration of the Yellow Stone, by Lieutenant Warren ; the Survey of Lieutenant Bryan ; the United States Naval Astronomical Expedition ; the North Pacific Behring Straits Expedition ; the Japan Expedition, and the Paraguay Expedition.

The Institution has also received, from other sources, collections of greater or less extent, from various portions of North America, tending to complete the government series.

The collections thus made, taken as a whole, constitute the largest and best series of the minerals, fossils, rocks, animals, and plants of the entire continent of North America, in the world.   Many tons of geological and mineralogical specimens, illustrating the surveys throughout the West, are embraced therein. There is also a very large collection of minerals of the mining regions of Northern Mexico, and of New Mexico, made by a practical Mexican geologist, during a period of twenty-five years, and furnishing indications of many rich mining localities within our own borders, yet unknown to the American people.

It includes, also, with scarcely an exception, all the vertebrate animals of North America, among them many specimens each of the Grizzly, Cinniman, and Black Bears ; the Panther, Jaguar, Ocelot, and several species of Lynx or Wildcat ; the Elk, the Mexican, Virginian, White-tailed, Black-tailed, and Mule Deer ; the Antelope, Rocky Mountain Goat and Sheep ; several species of Wolves and Foxes, the Badger, Beaver, Porcupine, Prairie Dog, Gopher, and also about seven hundred species of American Birds, four hundred of Reptiles, and eight hundred of Fishes, embracing Salmon, Trout, Pike, Pickerel, White Fish, Muskalonge, Bass, Redfish, &c.

The greater part of the Mammalia have been arranged in walnut drawers, made proof against dust and insects.   The birds have been similarly treated, hile the reptiles and fish have been classified, as, to some extent, have also been the shells, minerals, fossils, and plants.

The Museum hall is quite large enough to contain all the collections hitherto made, as well as such others as may be assigned to it.   No single room in the country is, perhaps, equal to it in capacity or adaptation for its purposes, as, by the arrangements now being perfected, and denoted in the illustration, it is capable of receiving twice as large a surface of cases as the old Patent Office hall, and three times that of the Academy of Natural Sciences of Philadelphia. When completely fitted, and specimens finally placed, the whole, taken together, will present a most imposing appearance.

Congress, in March, 1857, made an appropriation for the construction of suitable cases in the Smithsonian hall to contain the collection of the South Sea Exploring Expedition and others belonging to the Government. These will soon be transferred and appropriately arranged. The immense collection already in the Smithsonian Institution, although accessible to naturalists, and in constant use by them, has, for want of these cases, not been fully displayed to the public.

In the Museum hall may be seen a meteorite, the *largest* specimen in this country next to the Texas meteorite at Yale College.

It was brought to this country by Lieutenant Couch, of the United States Army, he having obtained it at Saltillo. It was said to have come from the Sancha estate, some fifty or sixty miles from Santa Rosa, in the north of Coahuila; various accounts were given of the precise locality, but none seemed very satisfactory. When first seen by Lieutenant Couch, it was used as an anvil, and had been originally intended for the Society of Geography and Statistics in the city of Mexico. It is said, that where this mass was found there are many others of enormous size; but such stories, however, are to be received with many allowances. Mr. Weidner, of the mines of Freiberg, states, that near the southwestern edge of the Balson de Mapimi, on the route to the mines of Parral, there is a meteorite near the road of not less than a ton weight. Lieutenant Couch also states, that the intelligent, but almost unknown, Dr. Berlandier, writes in his journal of the Commission of Limits, that at the hacienda of Venagas, there was (1827) a piece of iron that would make a cylinder one yard in length, with a diameter of ten inches. It was said to have been brought from the mountains near the hacienda. It presented no crystalline structure, and was quite ductile.

Prof. J. Lawrence Smith, of the Medical Department of the University of Louisville, gives the following account of this meteorite : "It weighs 252 pounds, and from several flattened places I am led to suppose that pieces have been de-

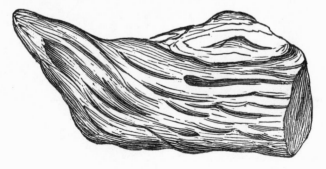

METEORITE FROM COAHUILA, MEXICO.

tached.   The surface, although irregular in some places, is rather smooth, with only here and there thin coatings of rust, and, as might be expected, but very feeble evidence of chlorine, and that only on one or two spots.   The specific gravity is 7.81.   It is highly crystalline, quite malleable, and not difficult to cut with a saw.   Its surface etched with nitric acid, presents the Widmannstättian figures, finely specked between the lines, resembling the representation we have of the etched surface of Hauptmannsdorf iron.   Schreibersite is visible, but so inserted in the mass that it cannot be readily detected by mechanical means.   Hydrochloric acid leaves a residue of beautifully brilliant patches of this mineral."

Prof. Smith, in a lecture on meteorites at the Smithsonian Institution, published in the Annual Report for 1855, advocates the theory of their *lunar* origin.

The Apparatus Room.

The Apparatus-room contains a large and valuable collection of instruments, prominent among which is the munificent donation of Dr. Robert Hare, of Philadelphia, who, when he resigned the Chair of Chemistry in the University of Pennsylvania, which he filled with honor to himself and his country for nearly thirty years, presented to the Smithsonian the instruments of research and illustration collected and used by himself during his long and successful scientific career.   The gift was important, not only on account of its intrinsic value, but also as establishing a precedent which should be frequently observed by others.   Besides the above, there is a full set of pneumatic instruments, of superior size and workmanship, constructed expressly for the Institution. by Mr. Chamberlain, of Boston; a set of ingenious

THE APPARATUS ROOM.

GERMAN STEAM ELECTRICAL MACHINE.

instruments for illustrating wave motion; a large electrical machine; Page's Electro-Magnetic instrument, &c., There is also in this room a large Fresnel Lens, such as is used in light-houses, and various instruments for the illustration of light, heat, sound, dia-magnetism, etc.

GERMAN STEAM ELEC-TRICAL MACHINE.

The Institution has just imported from Carlsruhe, Germany, a HYDRO-ELEC-TRIC machine which was constructed by C. Eisenlohr expressly to order. The effects which can be produced by this machine, are wonderful.

It consists principally of a tubular steam boiler resting upon glass columns, to secure insulation. The boiler is to be about two-thirds filled with the purest water, which is then heated, and the pressure of steam required is equal to six atmospheres. The steam at this high pressure is allowed to escape through very small openings. The electricity is thus produced by the friction of the particles of water against the inner surface of the orifices of the jet pieces, through which the steam issues. The least quantity of oil will destroy the friction, and prevent the development of electricity. This machine gives a constant succession of sparks, and charges a battery of sixteen large jars in thirty seconds.

HARE'S ELECTRICAL MACHINE.

In the apparatus-room, the most prominent object is a large electrical machine on an elevated platform.   This instrument was constructed by Dr. Robert Hare, of Philadelphia.

HARE'S ELECTRICAL MACHINE.

THE PICTURE GALLERY.

The Gallery of Art.

Besides a library, a museum, lectures, etc., among the earliest plans was the formation of a Gallery of Art, and, in accordance with this, a large room was devoted to this purpose. It was also determined that for the purpose of encouraging art, artists might exhibit their pictures here free of expense. The feature of this gallery is the very interesting series of portraits, mostly full size, of over one hundred and fifty North American Indians, with sketches of scenery, deposited by the artist who painted them, Mr. J. M. Stanley. These portraits were all taken from life, and are accurate representations of the peculiar features of prominent individuals of forty-three different tribes, inhabiting the Southwestern prairies, New Mexico, California, and Oregon. The faithfulness of the likenesses has been tested by a number of intelligent persons who have visited the gallery, and have immediately recognized among the portraits those of the individuals with whom they have been personally acquainted. The artist expended in the work of obtaining these pictures ten years of his life, and perseveringly devoted himself to the task in the face of difficulties and dangers which enthusiasm in the pursuit could alone enable him to encounter.

The catalogue of the pictures will be found in the appendix.

In this room is also deposited a marble statue, a copy of the celebrated work of art in Rome, the "DYING GLADIATOR." It was executed by an English sculptor, Jno. Gott.

Meteorological and Magnetic Observatory.

On the grounds near the Institution is a small building resembling a cottage, which is the above establishment. It principally consists, to secure an equable temperature, of an under-ground room, inclosed within two walls, between which a current of air is allowed to pass, in order to prevent dampness. It has been supplied with a set of apparatus for determining the continued variations in direction and intensity of terrestrial magnetism. By a very ingenious application of the photographic process, the invention of Mr. Brooks, of England, the instruments are made to record, on a sheet of sensitive paper moved by clock work, their own motions. First, to determine the variations of direction of the horizontal magnet; a steel bar, strongly magnetized, is suspended by several fibers of untwisted silk, so as to have perfect freedom of motion in the horizontal plane, and from a gas-light, kept perpetually burning, a single ray of light is thrown upon the concave mirror permanently attached to the magnetic bar, and consequently partaking of its movements. This ray of light is reflected and brought to a focus at the surface of a revolving cylinder, moved by clock work, on which the photographic paper is placed. When the magnet is at rest, the pencil of light is stationary, and consequently traces on the moving paper a simple straight line; but when the magnet is disturbed by the terrestrial perturbations, its oscillations are recorded by the motion of the pencil of light in a curved or zig-zag line.

To register the intensity or strength of the magnetic force, another bar magnet is suspended by two parallel silk threads, about an inch apart, descending from two hooks fastened to the under side of a plate attached to the ceiling, or some other support. The plate is then made to revolve through an arc of a circle, until, by the force of torsion, the magnet is deflected from a north and south to an east and west direction. It is thus kept in a state of equilibrium between the force of torsion of the threads, tending to turn its north end around still further to the south; and the magnetism of the earth, on the other hand, tending to bring it back to its north and south direction. If in this position the magnetism of the earth becomes stronger, it will prevail, and the north end of the needle will turn toward the north. If the magnetism of the earth diminishes in intensity, the force of torsion will prevail, and the same end will move toward the south. These motions, as in the case of the other magnet, are recorded by a beam of light on the paper surface of the revolving cylinder. But, besides the change of direction of the horizontal needle, a magnet, so supported as to be free to take any position, in this latitude will arrange itself with its end dipping toward the horizon. The amount of this dip, or variation, varies also in different places, and at different times; and to record these changes a bar is supported in the direction of the magnet north and south, on two knife edges, like the beam of a balance. Any change which takes place in the position of a magnet thus arranged is recorded by a mirror attached to the prolongation of the axes on which the bar turns.

It is proposed to keep these instruments constantly in operation, for the purpose of comparing results with observations of a similar character in different parts of the world; and also for the purpose of furnishing a standard to which the observations made at various points by the Coast Survey, and the different scientific explorations which are now in progress in the western portions of the United States, may be referred, and with which they may be compared.

On account of the delicate and peculiar nature of the apparatus employed, the Magnetic Observatory is not accessible to the public.

Observations are made at 7 A. M., 2 and 9 P. M. every day, of the barometer, thermometer, psychrometer, the direction of the wind, clouds, amount of rain, etc. These observations are carefully computed, together with those received from the Smithsonian corps of observers in every part of the country; and the material is thus accumulating for a valuable work on the meteorology of the United States. Blanks, instructions, and tables are furnished gratuitously to persons who will make observations. Instruments are supplied when requested, but at the expense of the parties ordering—the income of the Institution being, as yet, insufficient to meet such and other like desirable outlays.

THE GREAT BAROMETER.

The instrument noticed in the hall, near the entrance, is a Sulphuric Acid Barometer, constructed by James Green, 173 Grand st., N. Y., expressly for the Institution.

The glass tube is 240 inches long, and ¾ths of an inch in diameter, and is enclosed in a cylindrical brass case of the same length, and 2½ inches diameter. The glass tube is secured in the axis of the brass case by a number of cork collars, placed at intervals, which while they prevent all lateral displacement of the tube, enable it to be moved upwards and downwards for the adjustment of the zero-point.

The reservoir consists of a cylindrical glass bottle of four inches in diameter, with two openings at the top; one in the axis to admit the lower end of the long tube, which is tapered to about one-half of the general diameter, the other to transmit the varying pressure of the atmosphere.

The scale for reading the elevation is divided into inches and tenths, and by means of a vernier, moved by a rack and pinion, the variations can be measured to a hundredth of an inch, and estimated to a still smaller division.

The drying apparatus, placed between the external air and the interior of the reservoir, consists of a tubulated bottle with two openings, containing chloride of calcium, and connected with the reservoir by an india-rubber tube, by which arrangement the air is deprived of its moisture.

To ascertain the temperature of the column of the liquid, two thermometers are attached, one at the top and the other near the bottom.

The advantages of the use of sulphuric acid are

1st. That it gives off no appreciable vapor at any atmospheric temperature; and 2nd. That it does not absorb or transmit air.

A full account of this instrument is given in the proceedings of the American Association, for the advancement of science, published by Jos. Lovering, Cambridge, Mass., 1857, p. 135.

On the top of the high tower of the Smithsonian building, and also on the grounds connected with it, may be seen a number of RAIN GAGES.

Several forms of this instrument have been used, but the one which has been found the best, under all circumstances, is shown in the annexed fi gure.

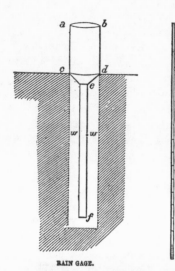

RAIN GAGE.

It consists of—

1. A large brass cylinder *a*, *b*, *c*, *d*, two inches in diameter, to catch the rain.

2. A smaller brass cylinder *e*, *f*, for receiving the water, and reducing the diameter of the column, to allow a greater accuracy in measuring the height.

3. A whalebone scale *s*, *s*, divided by experiment, so as to indicate tenths and hundredths of an inch of rain.

4. A wooden cylinder *w*, *w*, to be inserted permanently in the ground for the protection and ready adjustment of the instrument.

To facilitate the transportation, the larger cylinder is attached to the smaller by a screw-joint at *e*.

This instrument is made by James Green, New York, and is sold for $3 00. Several hundred of these gages have been distributed by the Institution and U. S. Patent Office.

On one of the towers may be seen an ANEMOMETER, or self-registering instrument, for denoting the direction and velocity of the wind. This apparatus was constructed for the Institution, by Dr. Charles Smallwood, of Montreal, precisely like one he has in use at his observatory in that city.

Exchanges.

The system of international exchange, planned and perfected by the Smithsonian Institution, has become very important in its results. In fact, it is now the principal medium of communication between the scientific and literary associations of the Old and New World. Lately the number of societies availing themselves of these facilities has largely increased—including, among others, nearly all the State Agricultural Societies of America, publishing transactions. This result has been produced by circulars which the Institution issued, to make this system more generally known Copious returns are being constantly received from the societies abroad; and an intercourse is thus established which cannot fail to produce valuable results, both in an intellectual and moral point of view. The packages from the Smithsonian are admitted duty free to all parts of the Continent of Europe—a certified invoice of contents by the Secretary being all that is required to pass them through the Custom Houses. On the other hand, all packages addressed to the Institution arriving at the ports of the United States, are admitted, without detention, duty free. Thus it will be observed that the system of exchange is the most extensive and efficient that has ever been established in any country. Its effects on our national character and reputation can scarcely be too highly estimated; for its influence, though silent, is felt in every part of the globe where science and literature are cultivated.

Several of the ocean steam navigation and a portion of our inland forwarding and transportation companies, in acknowledgment for the benefits they have received, as also to mark their high appreciation of the efforts of the Institution to promote knowledge, have carried the freight to and from Washington free of charge. We are pleased to record this fact, so honorable to the parties interested, and trust all their co-laborers will speedily follow their excellent example.

The Publications.

In the first report presented by Professor Henry to the Regents, he urged as a leading feature of the operations of the Institution, the publication of memoirs and periodical reports, the result of the labors of those engaged in original research. The advantages of this plan were stated as follows :

" In the first place it will serve to render the name of the founder favorably known wherever literature and science are cultivated, and keep it in continual remembrance with each succeeding volume, as long as knowledge is valued. A single new truth, first given to the world through these volumes will forever stamp their character as a work of reference. The contributions will thus form the most befitting monument to perpetuate the name of one whose life was devoted to the increase of knowledge, and whose ruling passion, strong in death, prompted the whole bequest intended to facilitate the labors of others in the same pursuit

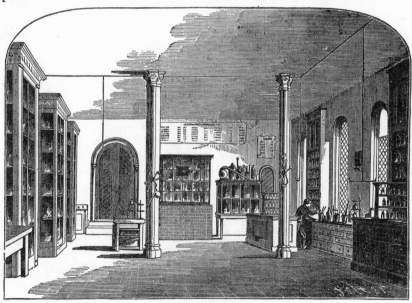

THE CHEMICAL LABORATORY.

"Again, the publication of a series of volumes of original memoirs will afford to the Institution the most ready means of entering into friendly relations and correspondence with all learned societies in the world, and of enriching its library with their current transactions and proceedings. But perhaps the most important effect of the plan will be that of giving to the world many valuable memoirs, which, on account of the expense of the illustrations, could not be otherwise published. Every one who adds new and important truths to the existing stock of knowledge, must be of necessity, to a certain degree, in advance of his age. Hence the number of readers and purchasers of a work, is often in the inverse ratio of its intrinsic value, and consequently authors of the highest rank of merit, are frequently deterred from giving their productions to the world on account of the pecuniary loss to which the publication would subject them. When our distinguished countrymen, Bowditch, contemplated publishing his commentaries on La Place, he assembled his family and informed them that the execution of his design would sacrifice one-third of his fortune, and it was proper that his heirs should be consulted on a matter which so nearly concerned them. The answer was worthy the children of such a father. 'We value,' said they, 'your reputation more than your money.' Fortunately in this instance the means of making such a sacrifice existed; otherwise one of the proudest monuments of American science could not have been given to the world. In a majority of cases, however, those who are most capable of extending human knowledge are least able to incur the expense of its publication. Wilson, the American ornithologist, states in a letter to Michaux, that he has sacrificed everything to publish his work. 'I have issued,' says he, 'six volumes, and am now engaged on the seventh; but as yet I have not received a single cent of the proceeds.' The following remarks, which are directly to this point, occur in an address on the subject of natural history, by one of the most active cultivators of this branch of knowledge: 'Few are acquainted with the fact that from the small number of scientific works sold, and the great expense of the plates, our naturalists not only are not paid for their labors, but suffer pecuniary loss from their publications. Several works on the different branches of zoölogy, now in the course of publication, will leave their authors losers by an aggregate of $15,000. I do not include in this estimate works already finished—one, for instance, the best contribution to the natural history of man, extant, the publication of which will occasion its accomplished author a loss of several thousand dollars. A naturalist is extremely fortunate if he can dispose of two hundred copies of an illustrated work, and the number of copies printed rarely exceeds two hundred and fifty."

The Smithsonian publications are presented to learned societies, public libraries, and other institutions in all parts of the world, and can be purchased by individuals, at about the cost of paper, printing, and binding. If circumstances admitted, the Regents would give a much more extended circulation to their publications; but their limited means prevent it. The fact must not be lost sight of that this is only one of their many operations. The cost of the publication by government of the Patent Office Report is more than quadruple the whole income of the Smithsonian Institution. Each memoir is printed separately, and with a separate title and paging, so that it can be distributed to persons most interested in its perusal as soon as it comes from the press, without waiting for the completion of the volume to which it belongs. In this way the author is enabled to present a full account of his discoveries to the world, with the least possible delay; while, by the rules of the Institution, he is allowed to publish an abstract of his paper in the proceedings of the American Association for the Advancement of Science, or in those of any properly organized society. The number of copies of the Smithsonian publications distributed is greater than that of the transactions of any scientific or literary society; and, therefore, the Institution offers the best medium to be found for diffusing a knowledge of scientific discoveries. Every memoir published is issued with the stamp of approval of a commission of competent judges; and, in order to secure a cautious and candid opinion, the name of the author, and those of the examiners are not made known to each other unless a favorable report is given; and in this case, the names of the commission are printed, as vouchers for the character of the memoir, on the reverse of the title page. This plan secures an untrammeled expression of opinion, while it induces caution on account of the responsibility which it involves.

RULES OF DISTRIBUTION.

The following rules have been adopted for the distribution of the quarto volumes of the Smithsonian Institution:

1. They are to be presented to all learned societies which publish transactions, and give copies of these in exchange to the Institution.

2. To all foreign libraries of the first class, provided they give in exchange their catalogues or other publications, or an equivalent in their duplicate volumes.

3. To all the colleges in actual operation in this country, provided they furnish in return, meteorological observations, catalogues of their libraries and their students, and all other publications issued by them relative to their organization and history.

4. To all States and Territories, provided there be given, in return, copies of all documents published under their authority.

5. To all incorporated public libraries in this country, not included in any of the foregoing classes, containing more than 7000 volumes; and to smaller libraries, where a whole State or large district would be otherwise unsupplied.

6. Separate memoirs are sometimes presented to minor institutions.

Correspondence.

There is one part of the Smithsonian operations that attracts no public attention, though it is producing, it is believed, important results in the way of diffusing knowledge, and is attended, perhaps, with more labor than any other part. This is the scientific correspondence of the Institution. Scarcely a day passes in which communications are not received from persons in different parts of the country, containing accounts of discoveries, which are referred to the Institution, or asking

3

questions relative to some branch of knowledge. The rule was early adopted to give respectful attention to every letter received, and this has been faithfully adhered to from the beginning up to the present time.

These communications relate to a great variety of subjects. Any topic which strongly excites the attention of the public at a given time, such as the announcement in the papers of a wonderful discovery, or an important invention which promises to introduce extensive changes in the useful arts, is sure to bring upon the Institution an increase of labor in the way of correspondence. The ordinary inquiries addressed to the Secretary relate to the principles of mechanics, electricity, magnetism, meteorology, names of specimens of plants, minerals, insects, and, in short, to all objects or phenomena of a remarkable or unusual character.

Requests are frequently made for lists of apparatus, for information as to the best books for the study of special subjects, hints for the organization of local societies, &c. Applications are also made for information by persons abroad relative to particular subjects respecting this country. When an immediate reply cannot be given to a question, the subject is referred, by letter, to some one of the Smithsonian co-laborers, and the answer is transmitted to the inquirer, either under the name of the person who gives the information or under that of the Institution, according to the circumstances of the case. In relation to this subject we quote from a recent report of Prof. Henry.

"There is no country on the face of the earth in which knowledge is so generally diffused as in the United States; none in which there is more activity of mind or freedom of thought and discussion, and in which there is less regard to what should be considered as settled and well-established principles. It will not, therefore, be surprising that the Institution should be called upon to answer a great number of communications intended to subvert the present system of science, and to establish new and visionary conceptions in its stead, and that numerous letters should be received pertaining to such objects as the quadrature of the circle, the trisection of the angle, the invention of self-moving machines, the creation of power, the overthrow of the Newtonian system of gravitation, and the establishment of new systems of the universe.

"Many of these communications are of such a character that, at first sight, it might seem best to treat them with silent neglect; but the rule has been adopted/ to state candidly and respectfully the objections to such propositions, and to endeavor to convince their authors that their ground is untenable.

"Though this course is in many cases attended with no beneficial results, still it is the only one which can be adopted with any hope of even partial good. In answering those who persist in declaring that the present received laws of mechanical action are erroneous, and that they have discovered new and more correct generalizations, they are requested to prove the truth of their assertions by predicting new and important phenomena, the existence of which may be immediately tested either by experiment or observation. It is not enough that the new system explains facts which we know, for this would be merely exhibiting old knowledge under a new form, but it should point out in the way of deduction new facts which have hitherto escaped the eye of the observer or the scrutiny of the experimenter.

"It is to be regretted that so many minds of power and originality in our country should, from defective scientific training, be suffered to diverge so widely from the narrow path which alone leads to real advance in positive knowledge. Providence, however, seems in some measure to vindicate the equality of its distributions, by assigning to such, a double measure of hope and self-esteem, which serves them instead of success and reputation."

"The faithful attention to the correspondence of the Institution, imposes a serious labor on the Secretary and his assistants. Beside the correspondence above mentioned, there is that which relates to the reception and publication of the memoirs; to the lectures; to particular branches of research; to the almost innumerable inquiries as to the character of the Institution; to applications for its publications; to the printing, engraving, binding, transportation, payment of accounts; and to the exchanges of the "Contributions to Knowledge."

"All the letters received are bound in volumes, and a copy of every answer is carefully preserved, the whole thus forming a permanent record of all the transactions of the Institution, as well as a history of the topics of scientific interest which have particularly occupied the public mind during any given period. The exposition of this labor, which has been increasing from year to year, will be a sufficient answer to the question which is sometimes asked, as to what the officers of the Institution find to do."

The Lectures.

With reference to this part of the operations of the Institution, the Secretary has presented the following views in his reports:

"Public lectures have become one of the characteristics of the day, and next to the press perhaps tend, more than any other means of diffusing knowledge, to influence the public mind. The liberal price paid by the Lowell Institute, and some of the associations in our large cities, induces men of reputation to devote themselves to the preparation of popular lectures. In some parts of the country a number of adjacent cities or villages enter into an arrangement by which the same lecture may be repeated, in succession, at each place; and in this way the amount paid becomes sufficient to call forth the best talent. Popular lectures appear better adapted to present literary and historical facts, and to give information relative to subjects of art and of morals, than to impart a knowledge of scientific principles. These require more attention and continuous thought than can be generally expected from a promiscuous audience. Hence the scientific lecturer frequently aims at a brilliant display of experiments, rather than to impress the mind with general principles.

"Local lectures are too limited in their influence to meet a proper interpretation of the will of Smithson; yet they were ordered by Congress, and are calculated to do more good in this city than in any other part of the Union.

"In selecting lecturers, the consideration of mere popular effect has not been re garded. The persons chosen have been such as to give weight to the lecture, and to reflect credit on the Institution. The object has been to give instruction rather than amusement—to improve the public taste rather than to elicit popular applause. The Institution, to be respected, must maintain a dignified character, and seek rather to direct public opinion than to obtain popularity by an opposite course.

"The moral effect which the lectures have on the city of Washington cannot be otherwise than beneficial. When the weather is favorable, the room is every evening crowded before the hour of commencement with an intelligent audience. The lecturers have generally been persons from a distance, who have expressed surprise to find such a large and respectful attendance in a city which is commonly thought to be exclusively devoted to politics and amusement. The plan of inviting gentlemen of reputation and influence from a distance, renders the Smithsonian operations familiar to those best qualified to appreciate their value, and best able to give a correct account of the character of the Institution in their own districts of country, as well as to vindicate its claims to the confidence and friendly regard of the public. The results of this course, and the distribution of the volumes of Contributions to colleges and public libraries, it is hoped, will so establish the Institution in the good opinion of the intelligent and influential part of the community, that it may bid defiance to the assaults of those who are ignorant of its true character, or are disappointed in not sharing its honors without the talents or the industry to win them."

The Secretary.

PROFESSOR HENRY.

In the report of the Committee on Organization, of the first Board of Regents, January 25, 1847, the nature of the duties of the Secretary are set forth, and the importance of his position duly considered. It is stated that inasmuch as the Chancellor being a Regent, can receive no salary for his services, it results almost necessarily that the Secretary should become its chief executive officer. The charter seems to have intended that he should occupy a very responsible position; granting as it does to the Secretary, in conjunction with the Chancellor, the power to determine the necessity and the amount of appropriations made for the purposes of the Institution.

The Committee stated that in their opinion "upon the choice of this single officer, more probably than on any one other act of the Board, will depend the future good name, and success, and usefulness of the Smithsonian Institution."

One of the first resolutions adopted by the Board of Regents was the following:

"*Resolved,* That it is essential for the advancement of the proper interests of the trust, that the Secretary of the Smithsonian Institution be a man possessing weight of character, and a high grade of talent; and that it is further desirable that he possess eminent scientific and general attainments; that he be a man capable of advancing science and promoting letters by original research and effort, well qualified to act as a respected channel of communication between the Institution and scientific and literary individuals and societies in this and foreign countries: and, in a word, a man worthy to represent, before the world of science and of letters, the Institution over which this Board presides."

It was with these feelings and opinions that the Board of Regents selected Professor JOSEPH HENRY, of the College of New Jersey, Princeton, to fill the office of Secretary. He accepted the appointment, entered at once upon his laborious and responsible duties, and has since given to them all his time and thoughts.

The views he held were not at first generally understood, but they are now appreciated and concurred in by those who have examined the subject, and who believe that Smithson did not intend to limit the influence of his bequest to one locality or nation, but designed, as is well expressed in the words of John Quincy Adams, "*to spread the benefits to be derived from the Institution not only over the whole surface of this Union, but throughout the* CIVILIZED WORLD."

The Grounds.

The grounds around the building were laid out by the distinguished horticulturist and landscape gardener, Downing, but he died while engaged in the prosecution of his plans.

We are indebted to the editor of the "Rural New Yorker," for the following remarks relative to this subject, and for the representation of the marble monument recently erected to his memory:

When the sad tidings of the death of Andrew Jackson Downing was announced, many hearts were stricken, and many countenances saddened. Every lover of rural life and rural taste, felt that a friend, a brother, and a leader had fallen. The homes of hundreds, from the foundation stone to the gable point, spoke of the departed— even the trees and flowers of the garden, told a tale of sadness. The furniture in our parlors, the books in our libraries, spoke too plainly to our wounded hearts of the loved and lost. Scarcely a city or village in our country but presented some monument of his skill and taste, something to remind the people how great and irreparable was their loss—cottages whose simple yet elegant adornings taught how truly *taste* may be independent of wealth; windows tempting the eye from loveliness within, to the glorious prospect without; stately trees that seemed to guard like sentinels the sacred precincts of home, and village churches whose walls

and spires spoke of religion to the heart.
It was at once proposed, in all parts
of the country, by Horticultural and
other Societies, that some suitable monument should be erected to the memory
of Mr. Downing, and in 1852, the
American Pomological Society ap-
pointed a committee to superintend this
work. The design adopted by the committee was furnished by Calvert Vaux,
of Newburgh, N. Y., the late partner
of Mr. Downing, and the work executed
by Robert Launitz, an eminent sculptor
of New York. The monument was
erected in the grounds of the Smithsonian Institution, at Washington, and it is
worthy of remark, that Mr. Downing
was engaged in laying out and beautify-
ing these grounds at the time of his death.
The committee made their final report
at the Pomological meeting in Sep-
tember, 1856. The funds were supplied
by friends of Mr. Downing, in Philadelphia, Newburgh, Boston, Washington,
Louisville, Buffalo, and Rochester.

The principal design of the monument
consists in a large vase resting on a pedestal, the whole executed of the finest
Italian marble. The pattern of the vase
is taken from an antique of the chastest
school. The vase is four feet in height,

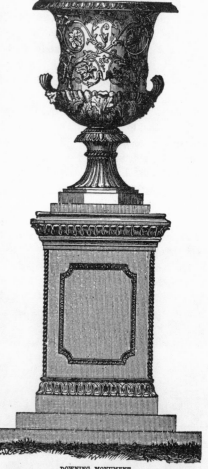

DOWNING MONUMENT.

and measures three feet in diameter on its upper rim. The body is ornamented
with rich arabesque; acanthus leaves surround the lower part. The handles
rest on heads of satyrs, (the tutelar gods of groves and woods.) The pedestal,
resting on a carved base, and being surmounted with a carved cornice, has on each
side deep panels, relieved by carved mouldings. Each of the panels contains
an inscription; that upon the Northern Front reads as follows:

THIS VASE
Was erected by his Friends
IN MEMORY OF
ANDREW JACKSON DOWNING,
Who died July 28, 1852, aged 37 years.

He was born, and lived,
And died upon the Hudson River.

His life was devoted to the improvement of the national taste
in rural art,
an office for which his genius and the natural beauty amidst
which he lived had fully endowed him.
His success was as great as his genius, and for the death of few
public men,
was public grief ever more sincere.
When these grounds were proposed, he was at once
called to design them ;
but before they were completed he perished in the wreck of the
steamer Henry Clay.
His mind was singularly just, penetrating, and original.
His manners were calm, reserved, and courteous.
His personal memory
belongs to the friends who loved him ;
his fame to the country which honored and laments him.

Inscription upon the Southern Front :

" The taste of an individual,
as well as that of a nation, will be in direct proportion to the
profound sensibility
with which he perceives the beautiful in natural scenery."

" Open wide, therefore,
the doors of your libraries and picture galleries,
all ye true republicans !
Build halls where knowledge shall be freely diffused among men,
and not shut up within the narrow walls of
narrower institutions.
Plant spacious parks in your cities,
and unclose their gates as wide as the gates of morning to the
whole people."

[*Downing's Rural Essays.*

Upon the Eastern Front is inscribed :

" Weep no more,
For Lycidus your sorrow is not dead,
Sunk though he be beneath the wat'ry floor,
So sinks the day-star in the ocean bed,
And yet anon repairs his drooping head,
And tricks his beams, and with new spangled ore
Flames in the forehead of the morning sky ;
So Lycidus sunk low, but mounted high
Through the dear might of Him that walked the waves."

Upon the Western Front is this Inscription :

I climb the hill from end to end,
Of all the landscape underneath
I find no place that does not breathe
Some gracious memory of my friend.

' Tis held that sorrow makes us wise,
    Yet how much wisdom sleeps with thee,
    Which not alone had guided me,
But served the seasons that may rise ;

And doubtless unto thee is given
    A life that bears immortal fruit,
    In such great offices as suit
The full grown energies of Heaven.

And love will last as pure and whole
    As when he loved me here in time,
    And at the spiritual prime
Re-waken with the dawning soul.

On the Base of the Pedestal is the following :

THIS MEMORIAL
Was erected under a resolution passed at Philadelphia,
in Sept., 1852, by the
AMERICAN POMOLOGICAL SOCIETY,
of which Mr. Downing was one of the
original founders.

MARSHALL P. WILDER, *President.*

The whole monument with its granite plinth is nine feet four inches in height, and cost $1,600.

Views from the Tower.

From the top of the highest tower, a magnificent, and by far the finest view of Washington and surrounding country is presented to the spectator. The city extends from northwest to southeast about four miles and a half; and from northeast to southwest about two miles and a half. Its circumference is fourteen miles. The avenues, streets, and open spaces, contain 3,604 acres, and the public reserva-tions 513 acres. The city is encompassed by a fine range of hills, forming a natural amphitheatre and covered in part with trees and underwood.

The following are the principal objects that present themselves to the view :

On the west is seen the Washington Monument, which has now reached a height of 175 feet. Further on, is seen the National Observatory, which is two miles from the Capitol. Georgetown, with its churches, college, &c., are seen in the distance to the northwest, and nearer are the President's House, the Treasury Department with its colonnade, on the right, and " Winder's building" used by the Pension Office and by bureaus of the War and Navy Departments, to the left.

Columbia College may be seen on one of the most commanding eminences of the hills at the north of the city, and a little to the east the marble tower of the new U. S. Military Asylum is plainly visible. The tall and beautiful steeple of the 5th Baptist Church, and also the spire of the Catholic Church, will be observed in the north.

The observer will recognize the Patent office and General Post office to the northeast.

The City Hall and Unitarian Church, both of yellow color, and Trinity Episcopal Church, built of red sandstone similar to that used in the Smithsonian edifice, are at the northeast.

Directly east is the Capitol of the United States, its magnificent proportions and commanding position constituting it the most prominent as it is the most interesting object in the landscape.

At the southeast are seen the ship houses and tall chimneys of the Navy Yard, and more towards the south on the neck of land at the junction of the Anacostia or East branch with the Potomac, are the Arsenal and the Penitentiary.

The Potomac river lies along the south of the city, and adds greatly to the beauty of the view. Alexandria, a city of 10,000 inhabitants, can be seen about six miles to the south.

At the southwest is the Long Bridge which connects Washington with Virginia, and on the commanding position, elevated more than 200 feet from the river is Arlington, the residence of George Washington Parke Custis, Esq.

THE GATEWAY.

CATALOGUE

OF

PORTRAITS OF NORTH AMERICAN INDIANS,

WITH SKETCHES OF SCENERY, ETC.

PAINTED BY J. M. STANLEY.

The collection embraced in this Catalogue comprises accurate portraits painted from life, of forty-three different tribes of Indians, obtained at the cost, hazard, and inconvenience of a ten years' tour through the South-western Prairies, New Mexico, California, and Oregon. The descriptions are by Mr. Stanley himself.

1.—CO-WOCK-COO-CHEE, OR WILDCAT. (Painted Dec. 1842.)

A Seminole Chief, and one of the most celebrated of his tribe; possessed of much vanity and an indomitable spirit, he has won for himself an exalted name and standing among his people.

At the outbreak of the Florida war, he was a mere boy; but he shouldered his rifle, and fought with so much courage and desperation, that he was soon looked up to as a master-spirit. This gathered a band of warriors about him, who adopted him as their chief leader. At the head of this party he became a formidable enemy of the United States troops, and gave them much trouble during that campaign, and probably would never have fallen into the hands of the whites, had he been able to procure food and ammunition for his band: being reduced to a state of starvation, he was obliged to surrender, and, by treaty stipulations with the United States Government, was with his people removed west of the Mississippi.

2.—AL-LECK TUSTENUGGEE. (Painted Dec. 1842.)

This chief is at the head of the Mikasukie band, and during the Florida war was one of the most active among the Seminoles.

3.—NOKE-SUKE TUSTENUGGEE. (Painted Dec. 1842.)

A Seminole Sub-chief of the Mikasukie band. A warrior of distinction, and Al-leck Tus-tenuggee's aid.

4.—AL-LECK TUSTENUGGEE, NOKE-SUKE TUSTENUGGEE, CUDJO, and GEO. W. CLARKE. (Painted Dec. 1842.)

Cudjo is a negro Interpreter, who served the United States during the Florida War; and Geo. W. Clarke is Seminole Agent.

5.—TUSTENUGGEE CHOP-KO, OR THE BIG WARRIOR. (Painted Dec 1842.)

A Seminole Mikasukie Sub-chief, and one of the most distinguished warriors of his tribe. He is six feet three inches in height, and well proportioned, and is esteemed one of the best ball players among his people. His countenance indicates any thing but intelligence or shrewdness; on the contrary, it exhibits evidence of a capacity to commit any act, however cruel and atrocious, at the bidding of his chief.

6.—CHO-CO-TE TUSTENUGGEE, (Painted Dec. 1842.)

A Sub-chief, of some note as a warrior, but abandoned and dissipated; he is painted in the costume in which he presented himself, with a bottle of "fire water" in his hand. He possesses an amiable disposition, and is passionately fond of joking, which has acquired for him the celebrity of punster to the band.

7.—HAL-BURTA-HADJO, OR ALLIGATOR. (Painted Aug., 1843.)

A Seminole Chief, celebrated for his prowess as a warrior. His name has been frequently before the public, as the instigator and perpetrator of many atrocious murders, during the Florida campaign. He has suffered much from sickness since his removal, and looks dejected and careworn.

8.—COT-SA OR TIGER. (Painted Dec., 1843.)

A Seminole Warrior, and son of Alligator.

9.—SEM-I-WOC-CA. (Painted Sep., 1843.)

Represented as about crossing a small stream, with a corn-basket under her arm. She is attired in the costume peculiar to the Creek and Seminole women. Their dress consists of calico, of a coarse, cheap kind, worked to the depth of from twelve to fifteen inches from the bottom with different colors, in various devices.

The artist found it exceedingly difficult to get the women of this tribe to sit for their pictures, owing to the opposition of their chiefs, who do not consider them worthy of such an honor.

10.—OPOETH-LE-YO-HOLO. (Painted July, 1843.)

Speaker of the Upper Creeks. This man holds the rank of principal counsellor, or speaker of the councils, over which he presides with great dignity. His influence is so great, that questions submitted to the council are generally decided according to his will ; for his tribe consider him as the organ of their chief, and suppose he only speaks as he is directed.

11.—OPOETH-LE-YO-HOLO. (1843.)

Represented in the manner in which he paints himself when going to war. One would hardly recognize this celebrated chief in this disguise. He insisted on being thus painted, and it was with difficulty that he was afterwards induced to wash his face, and sit for a portrait which his friends would be able to recognize. See No. 10.

12.—A CREEK BUFFALO DANCE. (Painted Aug., 1843.)

This dance is enacted every year during the season of their busk, or green-corn dances ; and the men, women, and children all take an active part in the ceremony. They invest themselves with the scalp of the buffalo, with the horns and tail attached, and dance about. in a circle, uttering sounds in imitation of the animal they represent, with their bodies in a half-bent position, supporting their weight upon their ball-sticks, which represent the forelegs of the buffalo.

13.—TUSTENUGGEE EMATHLA. (Painted June, 1843.)

This is a fine looking man, six feet and one inch in height, and well proportioned, of manly and martial appearance and great physical strength, and is well calculated to command the respect of a band of savage warriors. He is generally known by the name of Jim Boy. Tustenuggee means "warrior;" and Emathla, "next to the warrior."

He is and always has been a firm and undeviating friend of the whites: he led a party of seven hundred and seventy-six warriors to Florida, and endeavored, first as mediator, to induce the Seminoles to abandon the bloody and fruitless contest in which they were engaged, but was unsuccessful.

14.—TO-MATH-LA-MICCO, OR THE LITTLE KING. (Painted June, 1843.)

Principal Chief of the Upper Creeks. Distinguished only as a warrior, he was elected to the chieftainship through the instrumentality of Opoeth-le-yo-holo, who has great influence over him. He is painted in the attitude of holding a red stick, which is invariably carried by him during the ceremonies of the busk or green-corn dance.   It is emblematical of the red-stick or late Creek war.

Possessing no merit as an orator or counsellor, his will is easily swayed by his speaker. He is mild and amiable in his disposition, and much beloved by his people.

15.—TUCK-A-BACK-A-MICCO, OR THE MEDICINE-MAN OR PHYSIC-MAKER. (Painted June, 1843.)

This is the great Medicine or Mystery Man of the Creeks; his fields of corn are cultivated by the people of the town in which he resides, and a salary of five hundred dollars per annum is allowed him from the treasury of the nation, for his services.

They suppose him to be indued with supernatural powers, and capable of making it rain copiously at will.

In his town is a building of rather a singular construction, used during their annual busk or green-corn dances as a dancing-house.   It is of a circular form, about sixty feet in diameter and thirty feet high, built of logs; and was planned by this man in the following manner:

He cut sticks in miniature of every log required in the construction of the building, and distributed them proportionately among the residents of the town, whose duty it was to cut logs corresponding with their sticks, and deliver them upon the ground appropriated for the building at a given time.   At the raising of the house, not a log was cut or changed from its original destination; all came together in their appropriate places, as intended by the designer.   During the planning of this building, which occupied him six days, he did not partake of the least particle of food.

16.—TAH-COO-SAH-FIXICO, OR BILLY HARDJO. (Painted Aug., 1843.)

Chief of one of the Upper Creek towns.   He is a merchant or trader among his people; also, has an extensive farm and several negro slaves, which enable him to live very comfortably.   He is much beloved and respected by his people.   The dress in which he is painted is that of a ball-player, as they at first appear upon the ground.   During the play they divest themselves of all their ornaments, which are usually displayed on these occasions, for the purpose of betting on the result of the play: such is their passion for betting, that the opposing parties frequently bet from five hundred to a thousand dollars on a single game.

17.—CHILLY McINTOSH. (Painted June, 1843.)

An Upper Creek Chief.   This man is a brother of Gen. McIntosh, who was killed some years since by his people, for negotiating a treaty with the United States Government, contrary to the laws of his country.   Chilly was pursued by the same party who massacred his brother, but succeeded in making his escape by swimming a river, which arrested his pursuers.

18.—KEE-SEE-LAH AND AH-SEE-HEE. (Painted Aug., 1843.)

Daughters of Opoeth-le-yo-holo.   The latter is commonly denominated the Young Queen. The remaining figure on the right is a half-breed and the wife of a white trader.

19.—COO-WIS-COO-EE, OR JOHN ROSS. (Painted Sept., 1844.)

Principal Chief of the Cherokees.   Mr. Ross has been for a number of years at the head of his people, which fact is sufficient evidence of the high estimation in which they hold him as a man capable of discharging the responsible duties devolving upon the office.   Mr. R: is a man of education, and as a statesman would do honor to the legislative halls of any country.   His hospitality is unbounded; from his soft and bland manners, his guests are at once made to feel at home, and forget that they are far from the busy scenes of civilization, and surrounded by the red men of the forest.   His house is the refuge of the poor, starved, and naked Indian; when hungry, he is sure to find at the abode of this exemplary man something wherewith to appease his hunger, and if naked, a garment to cover his nakedness.

Of his private and political history much might be said ; but we leave it to those who are more competent to the task, and able to do him that justice due to so eminent a man.

20.—KEETH–LA, or DOG. (Painted 1844.)

Commonly called Major George Lowry, Second or Assistant Chief of the Cherokees; an office which he has filled for a number of years with much credit to himself and the entire satisfaction of his people. He is about seventy years of age, speaks English fluently, and is an exemplary Christian.

He is painted in the attitude of explaining the wampum, a tradition of the manner in which peace was first brought about among the various Indian tribes. (See No. 27.)

21.—STAN WATIE. (Painted June, 1843.)

A highly gifted and talented Cherokee. This man is a brother of Boudinot, who was murdered some years since for his participation in negotiating with the United States the New Echota treaty, (which has caused so much internal dissention among the Cherokees,) contrary to the laws of his country. Stan Watie was also one of the signers of that instrument, but has thus far escaped the horrible death that befell his brother. He is reputed to be one of the bravest men of his people. During the session of the International Council, at Tah-le-quah, in June, 1843, he sat for his portrait; he was surrounded by hundreds of his enemies at the time, but did not manifest the least symptoms of fear during his sojourn. A biography of this man's life would form a very interesting volume.

22.—THOMAS WATIE. (Painted 1842.)

Brother of STAN WATIE, a fine-looking man, but abandoned and dissipated. He is a printer by trade, and speaks English fluently, and writes a good hand.

23.—YEAH-WEE-OO-YAH-GEE or THE SPOILED PERSON. (Painted 1844.)

This man was one of the signers of the first treaty made with the Cherokees by the United States Government, during the administration of General Washington.

24.—OH-TAH-NEE-UN-TAH, or CATCHER. (Painted 1844.)

A Cherokee Warrior.

25.—CHARLES McINTOSH. (Painted 1842.)

A Cherokee half-breed, about twenty-three years of age, little known among his people until December, 1842. He then distinguished himself by killing a man upon the Prairies, by the name of Merrett, an escaped convict from the jail at Van Buren, Arkansas, who with his brother was under sentence to the State Prison, had escaped, and fled to the Prairies, where they carried on a sort of land piracy, robbing and murdering all travellers whom chance threw into their power.

26.—WE-CHA-LAH-NAE-HE, or THE SPIRIT. (Painted 1844.)

Commonly called John Huss. A regular ordained minister of the Presbyterian denomination, and speaks no English. He is a very pious and good man.

27.—INTERNATIONAL INDIAN COUNCIL. (Painted 1843.)

This council was convened by John Ross, at Tah-le-quah, in the Cherokee Nation, in the month of June, 1843, and continued in session four weeks. Delegates from seventeen tribes were present, and the whole assemblage numbered some ten thousand Indians

28.—THREE CHEROKEE LADIES. (Painted 1842.)

29.—TWO CHEROKEE GIRLS. (Painted 1842.)

30.—CADDO COVE, CADDO CREEK, ARKANSAS. (Painted 1843.)

Gov. P. M. Butler and party on their return from the council with the wild Indians.

31.—VIEW OF THE ARKANSAS VALLEY FROM MAGAZINE MOUNTAIN. (Painted 1844.)

32.—NATURAL DAM IN CRAWFORD COUNTY, ARKANSAS. (Painted 1844.)

33.—VIEW OF DARDANELLE ROCK ON THE ARKANSAS. (Painted 1844.)

34.—ISH-TON-NO-YES, or JAMES GAMBLE. (Painted 1843.)

Chickasaw Interpreter. A young man of education, and speaks English fluently.

35.—WA-BON-SEH, or THE WHITE SKY. (Painted June, 1843.)

Principal Chief of the Prairie Band of Potowatomies, residing near Council Bluffs. This chief is a bold and sagacious warrior, but possesses no merit as an orator; his will is submitted to his people through his speaker, a man possessed of great powers of oratory.
Many of his war exploits are of a thrilling and exciting nature.

36.—OP-TE-GEE-ZHEEK, or HALF-DAY. (Painted June, 1843.)

Principal Speaker and Counsellor of the Potowatomies. This man is justly celebrated for his powers of oratory. By his dignity of manner, and the soft and silvery tones of his voice, he succeeds admirably in gaining the most profound attention of all within hearing. At the council which he attended in the Cherokee nation he attracted universal attention, both from his eloquence and the singularity of his dress, the style of which he probably obtained from the Catholic missionaries residing upon the frontier.

37.—NA-SWA-GA, or THE FEATHERED ARROW. (Painted 1843.)

Principal Chief of a band of Potowatomies, residing on the waters of Little Osage River; he is distinguished as a bold warrior.

38.—THOMAS HENDRICK. (Painted 1843.)

Principal Chief of the Stockbridges. Of this tribe but few are living, and they have united themselves with the Delawares, with whom they cultivate the soil in common. This man speaks good English, and is very affable in his manners.

39.—JIM GRAY. (Painted 1843.)

Principal Chief of the Munsees, a small tribe residing among the Delawares.

40.—SHAB-A-NEE. (Painted 1843.)

An Ottawa Chief. This man is well known throughout the northern part of Michigan and Illinois, his people having formerly occupied and owned the soil in that region. During the late war he was one of the most prominent actors, and one of Tecumseh's counsellors and aides-de-camp. He says he was near Tecumseh when he fell, and represents him as having been stabbed through the body with a bayonet by a soldier: he seized the gun with his left hand, raised his tomahawk, and was about to dispatch him, when an officer, wearing a *chapeau* and riding a white horse, approached him, drew a pistol from his holster, and shot him. He and the remaining few of his people reside with the Potowatomies, near Council Bluffs, on the Missouri.

41.—SAUSH-BUX-CUM, or BEAVER DRAGGING A LIMB. (Painted 1843.)

A Chippewa Chief. This man is chief of a small band of Chippewas, residing in Potowatomie country; these are more advanced in civilization than those living on the Northern Lakes; they are not unlike the Potowatomies in their manners and customs.

42.—CAPT. KETCHUM. (Painted 1843.)

A Delaware Chief.

43.—SECOND EYE. (Painted 1843.)

A Delaware Chief.

44.—RO-KA-NOO-WHA, the LONG TRAVELLER. (Painted 1843.)

Commonly called Jim Second Eye, Head War-Chief of the Delawares.
Some years since, a small band of Delawares, while on a hunting and trapping expedition

on the upper Missouri, were surprised by a large party of Sioux, who fell upon them and murdered all but one of the party, who succeeded in making good his escape and return to his people. Second Eye immediately started with a small force to avenge the death of his warriors; after traveling several weeks, they fell in with the identical party who committed the depredation. The Sioux, anticipating an attack, retreated to a deep ravine in the mountains in order to defend themselves more advantageously. Second Eye, perceiving the many disadvantages under which he labored, but having an indomitable spirit, determined to surmount all obstacles, and obtain that vengeance which the death of his warriors loudly called for. He waited until all was quiet within the ravine, raised the war-whoop, rushed madly upon them, and massacred the whole party; he having with his own hands cut off the heads of sixteen Sioux, which he threw to his warriors to scalp.

He speaks some English, and is frequently employed by the United States and Texas as a "*runner*" to the wild Indians, with whom he carries on a very successful trade. He derives his name of Long Traveler from the fact that he has crossed the mountains to Oregon, and has visited Santa Fé, California, and the Navahoe Village.

45.—AH-LEN-I-WEES. (Painted 1843.)

A Delaware Warrior of distinction in his tribe.

46.—CAPT. McCALLAH. (Painted 1843.)

Principal Chief of the Texan Delawares. This man is very influential among his people; he also exerts a great influence over the wild Indians, and his presence is considered indispensable at all councils convened either by the United States or Texas, for the purpose of negotiating treaties.

47.—PA-CON-DA-LIN-QUA-ING, OR ROASTING EARS. (Painted 1843.)

Second or Assistant Chief of the Texan Delawares, and Principal Orator and Counselor.

48.—WAH-PONG-GA, OR THE SWAN. (Painted 1843.)

Principal Chief of the Weeahs. Once a powerful tribe, but now reduced to the small number of two hundred warriors. They formerly resided in Indiana, and are at present located with the Piankeshaws, about forty miles south of Fort Leavenworth, on the Missouri.

49.—QUAH-GOM-MEE. (Painted 1843.)

Principal Chief of the Shawnees.

50.—SHAC-EE-SHU-MOO. (Painted 1843.)

An hereditary Shawnee Chief.

51.—PAH-QUE-SAH-AH, OR LITTLE TECUMSEH. (Painted 1843.)

A son of Tecumseh. He has none of the extraordinary traits of character for which his sire was celebrated, and is of very little note in his tribe; he was in the battle in which his father fell.

52.—KEOKUK. (Painted May, 1846.)

Head Chief of the Sacs and Foxes. Keokuk is in all respects a magnificent savage. Bold, enterprising, and impulsive, he is also politic, and possesses an intimate knowledge of human nature, and a tact which enables him to bring the resources of his mind into prompt operation. His talents as a military chief and civil ruler are evident from the discipline which exists among his people.

This portrait was painted in the spring of 1846, on the Kansas River, where he, with his people, were temporarily residing after their removal from the Desmoines River.

53.—SAC CHIEF, AND FOX BRAVE. (Painted May, 1846.)

54.—KEP-PEO-LECK, OR RED WOLF. (Painted May, 1846.)

55.—SAC WAR CHIEF, IN WAR PAINT. (Painted May, 1846.)

56.—WIFE AND DAUGHTER OF BLACK HAWK. (Painted May, 1842.)

57.—MEDICINE DANCE OF THE SACS. (Painted May, 1846.)

The Medicine Dance of the Sacs is performed once every year, for the purpose of initiating the mystery or medicine-men into this sacred custom of their tribe.

58.—THE CHIEFTAIN'S GRAVE. (Painted, Jan. 1851.)

A form of burial practised by many tribes inhabiting the borders of Missouri and Iowa.

59.—FLIGHT OF A MOUNTAIN TRAPPER. (Painted 1851.)

The flight of a Mountain Trapper from a band of Black-Foot Indians, constitutes an incident in the life of Capt. Joe Meek, the present marshal of Oregon Territory.   He was a native of Ohio, and early in life enlisted in the service of the American Fur Company as a trapper; in which service he spent eighteen years in the Rocky Mountains.

This picture represents one of the many thrilling incidents in his life, characteristic of the trapper and pioneer.   Finding himself pursued by a large party, he hoped, by the aid of a well-bred American horse, to escape a personal encounter; but the Indians taking advantage of the broken country, soon overtook him, and were showering their arrows at him while in full pursuit, using their horses as a shield.   Joe, reserving his fire for a favorable moment, selected the war-chief who was foremost, and, with well-directed aim, hit both horse and rider, which caused them to abandon the pursuit.

Joe was one of the early pioneer residents of Oregon, and one of its first representatives under the provisional government.

60.—THE TRAPPER'S ESCAPE. (Painted 1851.)

Joe is seen in the middle ground of the picture, waving his gun in exultation at his lucky escape.

61.—BLACK FOOT INDIANS IN AMBUSH, AWAITING THE APPROACH OF AN EMIGRANT PARTY. (Painted 1852.)

A composition characteristic of Indian warfare.

62.—TECHONG-TA-SABA or BLACK DOG. (Painted 1843.)

Principal Chief of the Osages.   A man six feet six inches in height, and well proportioned, weighing some two hundred and fifty pounds, and rather inclined to corpulency.   He is blind of one eye.   He is celebrated more for his feats in war than as a counselor; his opinions are, however, sought in all matters of importance appertaining to the welfare of his people.   The name Black Dog was given to him from a circumstance which happened when on a war expedition against the Comanches.   He, with his party, were about to surprise their camp on a very dark night, when a black dog, by his continued barking, kept them at bay.   After several ineffectual attempts, being repelled by the dog, Techong-ta-saba became exasperated, and fired an arrow at random, hitting him in the head and causing instant death.   By this name he is familiarly known to the officers of the army and white traders in that section of country

63.—SHU-ME-CUSS, or WOLF. (Painted 1843.)

A nephew of Black Dog, and a warrior of distinction among his people.

64—CROW-SUN-TAH, or BIG SOLDIER. (Painted 1843.)

An Osage Chief and Brave; is about seventy years of age, vigorous and active.   He together with a number of his tribe, were taken to France some years since by an American citizen for the purpose of giving exhibitions of their various dances.

65.—NE-QUA-BA-NAH. (Painted 1843.)

An Osage Warrior.

66.—CHA-PAH-CAH-HA, or EAGLE FEATHER. (Painted 1843.)

An Osage Warrior.   His head-dress is composed of the skin from the head of a buffalo, with the horns attached.

67.—THE OSAGE MIMIC. (Painted 1843.)

This picture is painted from an incident that took place in my studio at Tah-le-quah, in the Cherokee nation, during the session of the International Council, in 1843.

I was often absent for a short time, sketching, and listening to the various speeches made in council. My door being of rather a rude construction, fastened only by a common wooden latch, all Indians who chose had free ingress. Among those who paid me frequent visits, was an Osage boy, about seventeen years of age, by the name of Wash-cot-sa, an hereditary chief, possessed of an amiable disposition and inquiring mind. He seemed to observe every thing going on in my studio, and would endeavor to imitate any thing done by me. On one occasion I had been absent for a short time, and during the interim he and one of his companions sauntered in; and finding themselves alone, he concluded to try his hand at painting. He assumed the palette and brushes, placed his subject in a favorable position, and had made some few chalk-marks upon the canvass, when I entered; he immediately discovered me, and, dropping the palette and brushes and pointing to the canvass, said it was *pe-shee* very bad. I endeavored to induce him to return to his work, but to no purpose.

68.—AN OSAGE SCALP-DANCE. (Painted 1845.)

All tribes of wild Indians scalp their captives, save the women and children, who are treated as slaves, until ransomed by the United States Government.

On returning from the scene of strife, they celebrate their victories by a scalp-dance. The chiefs and warriors, after having painted themselves, each after his own fancy, to give himself the most hideous appearance, encircle their captives, who are all placed together. Thus stationed, at a tap on their drums they commence throwing themselves into attitudes such as each one's imagination suggests as the most savage, accompanied by yells, for the purpose of striking terror into the hearts of their captives.

This picture represents the scalp-dance of the Osages around a woman and her child; and a warrior in the act of striking her with his club, his chief springing forward and arresting the blow with his spear.

69.—KI-HIC-CA-TE-DAH, or PASSING CHIEF. (Painted 1843.)

Principal Chief of the Quapaws. Once a very powerful and warlike tribe, but now reduced to a small number; they reside with the Senecas. This chief is represented by the agent as being a very good man, and possesses the entire confidence of his whole people.

70.—WO-HUM-PA, an IOWA CHIEF, and the ARTIST. (Painted 1843.)

It was with much difficulty that I induced this chief to sit for his portrait. I was anxious to paint one of his warriors upon the same canvass with him; to this he objected, saying that they were *no good*, and that chiefs only were worthy of such a distinguished honor; he insisted on being painted in the act of shaking hands with me, so that when the Great Father (the President of the U. S.) saw it, he might know that he was a friend of the white man. He is a great warrior, his arms bearing evidence of this fact, having been pierced with balls and arrows in several places from the hands of the Sioux. He was very particular as to the correct imitation of the painting on his blanket, which is to him the history of his war exploits. • The hands represent the scalps taken from the heads of his enemies. I tried repeatedly to get some of his warriors to sit, but they could not be induced to do it without the consent of their chief. Such was their fear of him, that they dared not enter my studio while he was present without his invitation.

71.—KA-SA-ROO-KA, or ROARING THUNDER. (Painted 1842.)

Principal Chief of the Wichetaws or Pawnee Picts.

72.—NASH-TAW, or THE PAINTER. (Painted 1842.)

Second Chief of the Wichetaws or Pawnee Picts, and a brother of Ka-sa-roo-ka.

4

73.—RIT-SA-AH-RESCAT, or THE WOMAN OF THE HUNT, and BRACES or BABY. (Painted 1842.)
Wife of Nashtaw, and Child.

74.—BIN-TAH, THE WOUNDED MAN. (Painted 1843.)
Principal Chief of the Caddoes. He derived his name from the fact of his having been wounded in the breast by an Osage; he wears a piece of silver suspended from his nose, as an ornament.

75.—AH-DE-BAH, or THE TALL MAN. (Painted 1843.)
Second or Assistant Chief of the Caddoes. Painted in the act of striking the drum.

76.—SE-HIA-AH-DI-YOU, THE SINGING BIRD. (Painted June, 1843.)
Wife of Ah-de-bah, seated in her tent. A view on Tiwoccany Creek, Texas.

77.—HA-DOON-COTE-SAH. (Painted 1843.)
A Caddo Warrior.

78.—JOSE MARIA. (Painted 1844.)
Principal Chief of the Anandarkoes. This Chief is known to the Mexicans by the name of José Maria, and to the Caddoes as Iesh. He has fought many battles with the Texans, and was severely wounded in the breast in a skirmish with them.

79.—KA-KA-KATISH, or THE SHOOTING STAR. (Painted 1843.)
Principal Chief of the Wacoes. This man is justly celebrated for his powers of oratory, being probably one of the greatest natural orators now living among the Indians. At the council held upon the River Brazos, he was the principal speaker; and by his dignity and grace of manner succeeded in gaining the attention and respect of these wild and untutored sons of the forest, whose implicit confidence he enjoys.

80.—CHO-WE, or THE BOW. (Painted 1843.)
Principal Chief of the Natchitoches. This man had a brother killed by the Texans, some four or five years since, while on a hunting expedition, whose death he afterwards avenged by taking the scalps of six Texans.

81.—KEECHE-KA-ROOKI, or THE MAN WHO WAS NAMED BY THE GREAT SPIRIT. (Painted 1844.)
Principal Chief of the Towocconies, and acknowledged Chief of the allied tribes of Texas.

82.—KO-RAK-KOO-KISS. (Painted 1844.)
A Towoccono warrior.

83.—KO-RAN-TE-TE-DAH, or THE WOMAN WHO CATCHES THE SPOTTED FAWN. (Painted 1844.)
A Keechie Woman, wife of Ko-rah-koo-kiss.

84.—KOT-TAN-TEEK. (Painted 1844.)
Principal Chief of the Keechies.

85.—A BUFFALO HUNT. (Painted 1845.)
On the South-western Prairies.

86.—POO-CHON-E-QUAH-EEP, or BUFFALO-HUMP. (Painted 1844.)
Second Chief of the Hoesh Band of Comanches, and head war-chief of all the Comanches. This Chief was painted at a council of the wild Indians on the head-waters of Red River.

87—PO-CHON-NAH-SHON-NOC-CO, or THE EATER OF THE BLACK BUFFALO HEART. (Painted 1844.)
One of the principal warriors of the Hoesh Band, or Honey-Eaters.

88—WIFE OF PO-CHON-NAH-SHON-NOC-CO. (Painted 1844.)

89.—O-HAH-AH-WAH-KEE, THE YELLOW PAINT HUNTER. (Painted 1844.)
Head Chief of the Ta-nah-wee Band of Comanches.

90.—NAH-MOO-SU-KAH. (Painted 1844.)
Comanche Mother and Child.

91.—A COMANCHE DOMESTIC SCENE. (Painted 1844.)

A Sleeping Warrior. Landscape on the head-waters of Red River.

92.—A COMANCHE GAME. (Painted 1844.)

This game is played exclusively by the women. They hold in their hand twelve sticks about six inches in length, which they drop upon a rock; the sticks that fall across each other are counted for game : one hundred such counts the game. They become very much excited, and frequently bet all the dressed deer-skins and buffalo-robes they possess

93.—JOSE MARIA VIGIL ZUAZO. (Painted 1852.)

94.—CARLOS VIGIL, EX-GOVERNOR OF PUEBLO. (Painted 1852.)

95.—JUAN ANTONIO VIGIL. (Painted 1852.)

96.—JOSE AHAYEA. (Painted 1852.)

97.—JOSE DOMINGO HERURA. (Painted 1852.)

98.—BLACK KNIFE. (Painted 1846.)

An Apache Chief, reconnoitring the command of General Kearney on his march from Santa Fe to California.

99.—VIEW ON THE GILA RIVER. (Painted 1851.)

" About two miles from camp, our course was traversed by a seam of yellowish-colored igneous rock, shooting up into irregular spires and turrets, one or two thousand feet in height. It ran at right angles to the river, and extended to the north and south, in a chain of mountains, as far as the eye could reach.

"One of these towers was capped with a substance many hundred feet thick, disposed in horizontal strata of different colors, from deep red to light yellow. Partially disintegrated, and lying at the foot of the chain of spires, was a yellowish calcareous sandstone, altered by fire, in large amorphous masses. In one view could be seen clustered the Larrea Mexicanna, the Cactus, (King) Cactus, (Chandelier) Greenwood Acacia, Chamiza, Prosopis Odorata, and a new variety of Sedge.''

" For a better description of the Landscape, see the sketch by Mr. Stanley."—*Lieut. Col. W. Emory's report to the Secretary of War.*

100.—PIMO CHIEF. (Painted 1846.)

101.—PIMO SQUAW. (Painted 1846.)

102.—MARICOPA CHIEF and INTERPRETER. (Painted 1846.)

103.—SHASTE SQUAW. (Painted 1847.)

A slave to the Clackamus Indians.

104.—ENAH-TE, or WOLF. (Painted 1848.)

A young Umpqua Warrior.

105.—TE-TO-KA-NIM. (Painted 1848.)

Klameth Chief.

106.—ENISH-NIM. (Painted 1848.)

Wife of Te-to-ka-nim.

107.—YELSTO. (Painted 1848.)

A Callapooya.

108.—STOMAQUEA. (Painted 1848.)

Principal Chief of the Chinooks.

109.—TEL-AL-LEK. (Painted 1848.)

Chinook Squaw.

110.—QUATYKEN. (Painted 1848.)

111.—DR. JOHN McLAUGHLIN. (Painted 1848.)

Former Chief Factor of the Hon. Hudson's Bay Company, and founder of Oregon City.

112.—GOV. P. S. OGDEN. (Painted 1848.)

Hon. Hudson's Bay Company, Oregon.

113—OREGON CITY. (Painted 1848.)

114.—WA-SHA-MUS. (Painted 1847.)

Principal Chief of the Willamette Falls Indians.

115—MARY AND ACHATA. (Painted 1847.)

Willamette Falls Squaws. This group belongs to the great family of Chinooks, or Flat-Heads.

116—WILLAMETTE FALLS. (Painted 1848.)

117—CASINO. (Painted 1848.)

This Chief is one of the Tlickitack Tribe, and the principal Chief of all the Indians inhabiting the Columbia River, from Astoria to the Cascades. In the plenitude of his power he traveled in great state, and was often accompanied by a hundred slaves, obedient to his slightest caprice. The bands over whom he presided paid him tribute on all the furs and fish taken, as also upon the increase of their stock, to support him in this affluence.

He was the petted chief of the Hudson's Bay Company, and through him they are undoubtedly much indebted for the quiet ascendancy they always maintained over these tribes.

It is said that on visiting Fort Vancouver, his slaves often carpeted the road, from the landing to the fort, with beaver and other furs, a distance of a quarter of a mile ; and that on his return, the officers of the Hudson Bay Company would take the furs, and carpet the same distance with blankets and other Indian goods, as his recompense. He is now an old man, having outlived his prosperity and posterity, to see a once numerous people reduced to a few scattered lodges, which must soon disappear before the rapidly growing settlements of the adventurous pioneers.

118.—PEO-PEO-MUX-MUX, or YELLOW SERPENT. (Painted 1847.)

Principal Chief of the Walla-Wallas, commonly called by the Hudson's Bay Company, Serpent Jaune.

119.—TE-LO-KIKT, or CRAW-FISH WALKING FORWARD.

Principal Chief of the Cayuses, and one of the principal actors in the inhuman butchery of Wailetpu. Was hung at Oregon City, June 3d, 1850.

120.—SHU-MA-HIC-CIE, or PAINTED SHIRT. (Painted 1847.)

One of the chief Cayuse Braves, and son of Te-lo-kikt, and one of the active murderers of the Mission family.

121.—TUM-SUC-KEE.

Cayuse Brave. The great ringleader and first instigator of the Wailetpu massacre—was hung at Oregon City, June 3d, 1850.

122.—WAIE-CAT—ONE THAT FLIES.

Cayuse Brave and son of Tum-suc-kee. This man, though young, was an active participator in the massacre of Dr. Whitman, and committed many atrocities upon the defenceless captives. He escaped the ignominious death which awaited those not more guilty than himself.

123.

Massacre of Dr. Whitman's family at the Wailetpu Mission, in Oregon, 29th of November, 1847.

124.

Abduction of Miss Bewley from Dr. Whitman's mission.

125.—CASCADES OF THE COLUMBIA RIVER.

126.—SALMON FISHERY ON THE HEAD-WATERS OF THE COLUMBIA.

127.—MOUNT HOOD.—(OREGON.)

.28.—TIN-TIN-METZE. (Painted 1847.)

A Nez Percé Chief.

129.—KEOK-SOES-TEE. (Painted 1847.)

A Pelouse Brave.

130.—VIEW ON THE PELOUSE RIVER.

131.—PELOUSE FALLS.

This beautiful cascade is situated about nine miles from the junction of the Pelouse with Snake River, and is estimated at three hundred feet in height. According to an old tradition, the Great Spirit caused this barrier to rise, to prevent the salmon from passing to a band of Indians living on its head-waters, with whom he was displeased.

132.—VIEW IN THE CASCADE MOUNTAINS.

133.—VIEW ON THE COLUMBIA.

135.—THE ARTIST TRAVELING IN NORTHERN OREGON IN THE MONTH OF DECEMBER.

136.—VIEW OF MOUNT HOOD.

137.—CASCADES OF THE COLUMBIA.

138.—THE GREAT DALLES BASIN, AND VIEW OF MOUNT HOOD.

139.—SE-LIM-COOM-CLU-LOCK, OR RAVEN CHIEF. (Painted 1847.)

Commonly called Ugly Head. Principal Chief of the Spokanes, or Flat-Heads, residing on the waters of the Spokane River.

140.—KWIT-TEAL-CO-KOO-SUM. (Painted 1847.)

Big Star Chief, a medicine-man of the Spokanes. Whenever a person is sick, this tribe supposes that the spirit has left the body, and hovers invisibly in the air, until it can be charmed or brought back through the agency of the medicine-man. To accomplish this end, the patient is placed in a sitting posture, enveloped in a buffalo-robe, or other covering, having only the top of the head exposed.

The medicine-man then commences dancing and singing around the patient, gesticulating mysteriously, and often clutching in the air with his hands, as if in the act of catching something. The spirit is supposed to be attracted by the chant, and to hover near the aperture at the top of the lodge; and the dance is often continued for an hour before it can be caught. It is then pressed and rubbed, as the medicine-man pretends, through the patient's skull, whose recovery, if not soon effected, he supposes to be thwarted by his having caught the spirit of some other person; and it then becomes necessary to undo his work by setting it at liberty, and repeating the performance until the right spirit is caught.

141.—KAI-MISH-KON, OR MARKED HEAD.

Spokane Chief.

142.—KAI-ME-TE-KIN, OR MARKED BACK.

Spokane Brave.

143.—PA-SE-LIX.

Spokane Squaw.

144.—TIN-TIN-MA-LI-KIN, OR STRONG BREAST.

145.—HI-UP-EKAN.

Stony Island Brave.

146.—LAH-KIES-TUM.

Stony Island Squaw.

147.—SO-HA-PE.

Stony Island Brave.

148.—WAH-PUXE.

Chief of the Priest's Rapid.

149.—KO-MAL-KAN, OR LONG HAIR.

An Okanagan Medicine-man.

150.—SIN-PAH-SOX-TIN.

Okanagan Squaw.

151.—VIEW ON THE SPOKANE RIVER.

152.—J. M. STANLEY, THE ARTIST. Painted by A. B. Moore, 1851.

LIST OF INDIAN TRIBES REPRESENTED.

CATALOGUE OF INDIAN PAINTINGS

BELONGING TO THE

GOVERNMENT COLLECTION.*

1. STING IOWAY...
2. SHING-YAW-BA-WUS-SEN, *The Figured Stone*...
3. MISH-SHA-QUAT, *The Clear Sky*—Chippeway Chief..
   Painted by C. B. King from a drawing by Lewis, 1827.
4. PE-A-JUK—A Chippeway...(King from Lewis, 1827.)
5.
6. AM-EIQUON, *Wooden Ladle*..(King from Lewis, 1826.)
7. MO-NEE-KAW, *He who goes under ground*..
8.
9. TU-GO-NIS-CO-TE-YEH, *Black Fox*—Cherokee Chief................................(King, 1828.)
10. EESH-TAH-HUM-LEAH, *Sleepy Eye*—Sioux Chief, from the band called the Sipsetongs.
11. MOOS-E-OM-O-NEE, *The Walking Iron*—Wah-pee-ton Sioux......(By S. M. Charles, 1837.)
12. LA-KEE-TOO-ME-RA-SHA, *Little Chief*—Pawnee...(King, 1837.)
13. WAH-RO-NE-SAH, *The Surrounder*—Otoe...(King, 1837.)
14. WAH-KE-ON-TAW-KAH, *Big Thunder*—Chief of the Medana Kanton Sioux...(King, 1837.)
15. HAW-CHE-KE-ONG-GA, *He who kills Osages*—Missouri.................................(King, 1837.)
16. O-WAN-ICK-KOH, *Little Elk*—Winnebago...........................(A. Ford from Lewis, 1826.)
17.
18. —————, Chippeway Chief..................................(King from Lewis, 1827.)
19. GA-DE-GE-WE, *Spotted*—Second Chief of the Chippeways, 54 years old......(King, 1835.)
20. WAA-KANN-SEE-KAA, *Rattlesnake*—Winnebago........................(Ford from Lewis, 1826.)
21. NAA-GAR-NEP, *The one who sits at the head*—Chippeway Chief..(King from Lewis, 1827.)
22. [See 42.] GENERAL PUSH-MA-TA-HA—Choctaw Chief...
23. MENAWEE—A great Warrior and Creek Chief...
    This chief commanded the party that killed Gen. McIntosh, and was one of the few that saved themselves
    from the defeat at the Horse-shoe, by swimming the river, after being badly wounded in the head.
24. MISTEPE—Yoholo Mico's son, a Creek ....(King, 1825.)
25. NAA-SHE-O-SHUCK, *Roaring Thunder*—Sac of Mississippi, son of Black Hawk.
    (King, 1837.)
26. YOOSTO, *Spring Frog*..
27. YOHOLO-MICO—Creek Chief..(King, 1825.)
28. —————A Creek warrior...
29. —————A Chippeway Chief.....................................(King from Lewis, 1827.)
30. I-AU-BEANU—A Chippeway..(King from Lewis, 1826.)
31. PAH-GUE-SAH-AH—Son of Tecumseh...(Shaw.)
32. TAH-COL-A-QUOT—A Sac...
33. [See 77.] KEOKUK, *Watchful Fox*—Chiocook Sac..
34. PAW-A-SHICK, *To dash the water off*—A Fox Chief............................(Cooke, 1837.)
35. COL. JOHN STEDMAN or STIDHAM...King, 1825.)
36. WEA-MATLA—Seminole War Chief ....(King, 1826.)
37. KEE-SHESWA, *The Sun*—Fox warrior...(King.)

---

* These Paintings are arranged on the east and southeast walls of the Picture Gallery.

38. TAH-RO-HOU, *Plenty of meat*—Ioway...(King, 1837.)
39. AP-PA-NOOSE-O-KE-MAW, *A chief when a child*—Sac...............................(Cooke, 1837.)
40. CA-TA-NE-CAS-SA, *Black Hoof*—Shawnee Chief...
41. PAH-SHE-PAH-HOW, *Stabber*—First Chief of the Sankys; a Sac.......................(King.)
42. [See 22.] GENERAL PUSH-MA-TA-HAW—Choctaw Chief.................................
43.
44. KAI-POL-E-QUAH, *White-nosed Fox*—A Fox Chief..
45. KE-WA-DIN, *The North Wind*—Chippeway Chief....................(King from Lewis, 1827.)
46. WA-CHA-MON-NE, *Partisan*—Ioway...(King, 1837.)
47. WHESH-LAUB, *The Sweet*..(King from Lewis, 1826.)
48. TIA-MAH, *The bear whose scream makes the rocks tremble*—Fox Chief.....................
49. WAU-TOP-E-NOT, *The Eagle's Bill*—Fox..............................(King from Lewis, 1826.)
50. NAHETLUC-HOPIE, *Little Doctor*—Creek Chief.......................................(King, 1825.)

> The red spots on his dress mark the balls that he received when he was surprised in his hut. The three lower balls were lower than marked in the picture. The paint on the face is commemorative of the same event, as the blood ran from his nostrils and mouth.

51. COOSA-TUSTENUGGA—Creek Chief..(King, 1825.)
52. KEE-ME-ONE, *Rain*—A Chippeway ....(King, 1827.)
53. OPOTHLE-YOHOLO—Principal Chief of the Creek deputation to Washington in 1825.
                                                                            (King, 1825.)
54. AT-TE-COURE, *The Young Reindeer*—Chippeway Chief.............(King from Lewis, 1827.)
55. O-TYA-WA-NIM-EE-HEE, *Yellow Thunder*—Chippeway Chief.....(King from Lewis, 1827.)
56. A-NA-CAM-O-GUSH-IA—Chippeway Chief from Rainy Lake......(King from Lewis, 1827.)
57. WAA-KAWN, *The Snake*—Winnebago.................................(Ford from Lewis, 1826.)
58. HOO-WAU-NEE-KAW, *Little Elk*—Winnebago orator of the Car-ray-mau-nee family.
59. O-CHEE-NA-SHINK-KAA, *The man that stands and strikes*—Winnebago.
                                                                            (Ford from Lewis, 1826.)
60. PA-SHE-NINE, *The good marksman*—Chippeway Chief.............(King from Lewis, 1827.)
61. WA-HE-KANS-HE-KAI—Winnebago......................................(King from Lewis, 1826.)
62. WADTZ-HE-DOO-KAANA—Chief of the Winnebagos ....(Ford from Lewis, 1826.)
63. MI-CO-A-NA-PAS—Second Chief of Seminoles; owns 70 slaves........................(King.)
64. NO-WAY-KE-SUG-GA, *He who strikes two at once*—Otoe..........................(King, 1837.)
65. WAI-KEE-CHAI, *Crouching Eagle*—Sanky Chief; Fox...................................(King.)
66. CAW-TAA-WAA-BEE-TA, *The Snagled Tooth*..
67. YAH-HAJO, *Mad Wolf*—Creek Chief....................................(King, 1825.)
68. FOLKE-TUSTE-NAJO, *Craggy Black Clay*—Seminole War Chief.................(King, 1826.)
69. JOHR RIDGE—Cherokee Chief. Secretary to the Creek delegation to Washington, 1825.
                                                                            (King.)
70. SELOTA—Creek Chief; a distinguished warrior: fought under General Jackson.
                                                                            (King, 1825.)
71. TUSKIE-HU-TUSTENUGGE, *Little Prince*—Creek Chief.............................(King, 1825.)
72. JACK-O-PA, *The Six*—Chippeway Chief................................(King from Lewis, 1827.)
73.
74. LE-SHAW-LOO-LA-LE-HOO, *Big Chief*—Pawnee Loup ....(King, 1837.)
75. NAU-KAW, *Wood*—Of the Cor-ray-mau-nee family. Principal Chief of Winnebago deputation, 94 years old...
76. DON VINCENTE GUERRERO, former President of the Mexican Republic—a distinguished chieftain..
77. [See 33.] KEO-KUK, *Watchful Fox*—First Chief of Sankys.............. ....(King, 1829.)
78.
79. PEE-CHE-KER, *Buffalo*—Chief of Chippeways...
80. APAULI-TUSTENUGGE—Creek Chief..(King, 1825.)

81. Mou-ka-ush-ka, *Trembling Earth*—Sioux of Missouri; died in Baltimore Oct. 25, 1837
(Cooke, 1837.)
82. A-misk-quew, *The Spoon*—Menomina War Chief..(King.)
83. ————————A Chippeway Chief.................................(King from Lewis, 1827.)
84. Oloe, *Ox*—Mahara..
85. To-ca-cou, *He that gives the first wound*—Sioux of Missouri.................(Cooke, 1837.)
86. Ha-sa-za, *Elk's Horn*—Sioux of Missouri..(Cooke, 1837.)
87. Ammoi, *He that comes for something*—Yancton Sioux.............................(King, 1837.)
88. Mah-ne-hah-nah, *Great Walker*—Ioway Chief...(King.)
89. Pes-ke-lecaro—Chief of the Republican Panis.......................................
90. Au-pantan-ga, *Big Elk*—Mohas Chief; a great orator.................................
91. Man-chousia, *White Plume*—Kansas Chief.....................................(King.)
92. Terre-ki-tan-ahu..
93. Is-ca-ta-pe, *Wicked Chief*—Great Panis..(King.)
94. Chou-cape-otos, *Half Chief*...(King.)
95. A-she-au-kou, *Sunfish*—Sac Chief....................................(King, 1837.)
96. Mar-ko-me-ta, *Bear's Oil*...
97. Raut-che-waime...
98. [See 143.] Red Jacket—Seneca Chief..............................(King, 1828.)
99. Teus-qua-ta-wa, *Open Door*...
100. (Cooke.)
101. Ne-o-mou-ne, *Walking Rain*—Ioway..............................(King, 1837.)
102. Waa-pua-taa, *Playing Fox*—Prince of the Foxes.............(Ford from Lewis, 1826.)
103. Nau-che-wing-ga, *No Heart*—Ioway..(King, 1837.)
104. Pee-mash-ka, *Fox winding in his course*—Chief of the Foxes......................(King;)
105. Wah-bawn-see, *Causer of Paleness*—Principal Chief of the Potawotamies.(King, 1835.)
106. Wa-pella, *The Prince*—Fox...(King, 1837.)
107. Holato-mico, *Blue King*—Seminole War Chief...............................(King, 1826.)
108. We-ke-roo-tau, *He who exchanges*...
109. Cor-ba-map-pa, *Wet Mouth*—Chippeway Chief...............(King from Lewis, 1827.)
110. Ma-hong-ga—Osage...(King, 1830.)
111. Heho-tustenugge, *Deer Warrior*—Seminole Partisan War Chief.........(King, 1826.)
112. Es-me-boin—Chippeway Chief..(King from Lewis, 1827.)
113. Cut-taa-tase-tia—Fox...(Ford from Lewis, 1826.)
114. Pa-nan-se, *Shedding Elk*—Sac..(King, 1827.)
115. Catoouse—Chippeway Chief...(King from Lewis, 1827.)
116. ————————A Sioux Chief..
117. O-kee-ma-kee-guid, *The chief that speaks*—A Chippeway...........................
118. Governor Hicks—Head Chief of the Seminoles.................................(King, 1826.)
119. Waa-na-taa—Grand Chief of the Sioux..(King, 1826.)
120. Kis-te-kosh, *One leg off*—Fox brave......................................(Cooke, 1837.)
121. ————————A Fox Chief..(King from Lewis, 1826.)
122. Ocan-gee-wack—Chippeway Chief...................................(King from Lewis, 1827.)
123. Kai-kee-kai-maih, *All fish*—Chief of Sankys..(King.)
124. Ochio-Finico, (war name,) Charles Connello, (English name)—Creek Chief.
(King, 1825.)
125. She-tah-wah-coe-wah-mene, *The sparrow that hunts as he walks*—A Sioux......(King.)
126. Tshi-zhun-kau-kaw, *He who runs with the deer*—Of the Day-kau-ray family. Winnebago Chief..
127. Wau-kaun-hah-kaw, *Snake Skin*—Of the Day-kau-ray family........................
128. Artoway, Paddy Carr—Creek Boy..

129. No-DIN, *Wind*—Chief of Chippeways..(King.)
130. CHOU-MAN-I-CASE—Otoe, half chief; husband of Eagle of Delight............................
131. RANT-CHE-WAI-ME, MA-HA-KA, *Female Flying Pigeon, Eagle of Delight*......................
132. WA-EM-BOUSH-HAA—Chippeway from Sandy Lake...
133. MUCH-A-TAI-ME-SHE-KA-KAIK, *Black Hawk*..(King, 1837.)
134. IOWAY..
135. MAJOR TIMPOOCHY BARNARD—A Creek Chief.....................................(King, 1825.)
136. MAUCH-COO-MAIM—Ioway...(King from Lewis, 1826.)
137. KI-HE-GA-MAW-SHE-SHE, *Brave Chief*—Omahaw.................................(King, 1837.)
138. LEDAGIE—Creek Chief...(King, 1835.)
139. WE-KE-ROO-TAW, *He who exchanges*—Otoe...(Kiug, 1837.)
140. KAA-KAA-HUXE, *Little Crow* ....(King from Lewis, 1826.)
141.
142. TOMA-HAKE-TAKE, *The warrior who speaks first*.................................(1826.)
143. [See 98.] RED JACKET—Seneca Chief...
144. KEOKUK, *Watchful Fox*, and MU-SEN-WONT, son of Keokuk, *Long-haired Fox.*
                                                               (King, 1827.)
145. CHIPPEWAY SQUAWS...(1826.)
146. CHIPPEWAY SQUAW AND CHILD...............................(King from Lewis, 1827.)
147. TSCHUSICK...(King, 1827.)

OTHER PAINTINGS.

M. GUIZOT, the celebrated statesman of France, painted by Healy.
A BATTLE SCENE.
THE MASSACRE OF THE INNOCENTS.
A CARDINAL.
CAPTAIN JOHN EVANS.
A TURKISH SULTAN.

The Paintings in the Apparatus Room are rough sketches to illustrate lectures. The largest represents an ancient Indian mound near Marietta, Ohio; another the Mosque of St. Sophia, at Constantinople; another the English Houses of Parliament; and scenes in Egypt, Turkey, &c., &c.

LIST OF BUSTS DEPOSITED IN THE INSTITUTION.

ROGER B. TANEY,	JOHN MILTON,	WILLIAM NORRIS,
ROBERT FULTON,	BENJAMIN HALLOWELL,	CLARK MILLS,
STEPHEN DECATUR,	THORWALSDEN,	AMOS KENDALL,
JOEL BARLOW,	FRANCIS P. BLAIR,	MISS FAIRFIELD,
THOMAS JEFFERSON,	JOHN C. SPENCER,	MISS HAMPTON.
DANIEL WEBSTER,	MARTIN VAN BUREN,	

GUIDE TO THE MUSEUM.

Museums are collections of miscellaneous objects and relics capable of illustrating the distant or the past. The word is of Greek origin, and literally signifies a place sacred to the Muses—the patron deities among the ancients of the various arts and sciences.

The British Museum, the largest in the world, was opened to the public on the 15th of January, 1759, and is therefore a century old. It has been the recipient, however, of immense donations from the Government, and numerous bequests from individuals.

The collection now in the Smithsonian Institution is of very recent origin, and is remarkable for its extent and value, considering that no special appropriation has ever been made by the Government for its increase. All that has been done has been to pay the necessary expenses of keeping it in order, and for the preservation of the specimens. The objects have been chiefly collected under the direction of the officers of the various Exploring and Surveying Expeditions, and have formed only an incidental part of their duties. A large number, however, have been presented by the correspondents of the Institution.

The collections made by the U. S. Exploring Expedition under Capt. Wilkes, U. S. N., 1838–42, are supposed greatly to exceed those of any other of similar character ever fitted out by a foreign government, no published series of results comparing at all in magnitude with that issued under the direction of the Joint Library Committee of Congress.

A full list of all the Expeditions from which specimens have been received will be found in the Smithsonian Report for 1858, (page 52,) copies of which are furnished gratuitously by the Secretary to those specially interested in the subject.

In the arrangement of the specimens, strict scientific accuracy has been sacrificed to convenience, and this remark will apply to this work, which is intended only for the popular reader. Catalogues which will give descriptions and scientific names of all the articles of natural history, will be published in due time by the Institution. The student will find in the volumes of the Report of the Pacific Railroad and Mexican Boundary Surveys, especially, accurate accounts of most of the specimens here exhibited.

The notes in relation to the specimens are from the highest authorities—the reports of the various Expeditions having been consulted, as well as the guides to the British Museum, &c., &c.

☞ On entering the hall, turn to the left, and examine—

CASE 1.

This contains a number of interesting animals. No. 41 is the Prairie Wolf or Coyote, from the Colorado.

These animals are able to make an incredible amount of noise, which has no resemblance to the bark of a dog. They sneak about during the day, but at night there are no bounds to their impudence. They will steal provisions literally from under your nose. They do not attack men unless wounded.

Nos. 42, 43, 44, Foxes...45, Wolf...46, Common Fox...47, Jackall...48, Chili Fox...49 and 50, California Porcupine...51, Arkansas Fox...52, Egyptian Porcupine...53, Fox...54, Cross Fox...55, Cross Fox from Salt Lake...56, Prairie Wolf, Platte River...57, Fox of Tierra del Fuego, very bold and fierce...58, Fox...59, Gray Wolf...60, Gray Wolf, Platte River, the common Wolf of North America..61 and 66, Peccaries or Mexican Hogs. This animal is rarely found alone. It emits an odor like that of the skunk...62, 63, 64, and 65, Ant Bears, or Ant-eaters, from the Cape of Good Hope, etc.

The Ant-eaters are remarkable for their long cylindrical tongues, covered with a glutinous saliva, by means of which they entrap and devour the insects upon which they live. The tongue is nearly twice the length of the whole head and muzzle together, and when not extended is kept doubled up in the mouth, with the point directed backward. It is very slothful and solitary. The female bears but a single young one at a birth. They are very rare, and seldom seen even in their native regions. The Indians eat their flesh.

CASE 2.

Fishes.—Among these are the Sticklebacks, which the California Indians catch in summer, and dry for winter use.....Trout, or River Bass.....Sun fishes.

CASE 3.

Upper Shelf.—The many-colored Wrens of Chili...The Diamond Bird, very valuable on account of its skin...Robins from Australia...Blue Birds from India...Red-crested Manakin of Brazil. In the middle of the shelf is the Superb Warbler of Australia...The Gold-crested Wren...The Black Cock and the Crowned Cock of Malacca.

Middle Shelf.—Cocks from Malacca. Notice especially the Wild or Jungle Cock of Asia.

Lower Shelf.—The Silver Pheasant of China.

This Pheasant is remarkable for the extraordinary length of its tail feathers, which no visitor can fail to admire. This noble bird is considered a rarity even in Pekin, its native district being one of the coldest and most mountainous provinces of China.

English Pheasants...Australian Turkeys...The Argus Pheasant of Malacca...The Lyre-tailed Pheasant of Australia...The Helmeted Hornbill...The Rhinoceros Hornbill of Malacca.

This strange horny excrescence is in reality extremely light, being cellular. The Hornbills feed on mice, small birds, reptiles, &c., which, throwing them in the air and catching them in the throat, they swallow whole.

CASE 4.

Against the Wall.—Fishes from California, Mexico, &c.

CASE 5.

EAST SIDE—*Upper Shelf.*—Pigeons and Doves.

WEST SIDE—*Middle Shelf.*—Here are some of the choicest specimens in the whole Museum, and worthy of special attention. The rare Birds of British Guiana, South America: Among these, No. 6, the Bearded Manakin...9, Black Headed Creeper...5, Mocking Bird... 11, King Humming Bird. On another stand, notice No. 4, the Bell Bird, the rarest in the collection...No. 5, the Quya.....No. 12, Female Amethyst Humming Bird with nest.... No. 11, the Tucan...The Emerald, Sapphire, Longbill, and other Humming Birds.

There is no group of birds so interesting to the ornithologist or to the casual observer as the humming birds; at once the smallest in size, the most gorgeously beautiful in color, and almost the most abundant in species of any single family of birds. They are strictly confined to the continent and islands of America, and are most abundant in the Central American States. There are believed to be nearly 400 species. Their food consists almost entirely of insects. The humming, from which they derive their name, is produced by the whirring of the wings.

Middle Shelf.—The celebrated BIRD OF PARADISE from New Guinea...The Blue-Headed Shrike or Butcher Bird from the Phillippine Islands...Blue-Backed Shrike from India... Burmese Shrike from Malacca...Cayenne Shrike...Brazil Shrike...Black-throated Shrike from Feejee Islands...The Common Jay, &c.

Many years ago, when rice was dear in Eastern China, efforts were made to bring it from Luzon, where it was abundant. At Manilla there was, however, passed a singular law, to the effect that no vessel for China should be allowed to load with rice unless it brought to Manilla a certain number of cages full of the little "butcher birds," well known to ornithologists. The reason for this most eccentric regulation simply was that the rice in Luzon suffered much from locusts, and these locusts were destroyed in great numbers by butcher birds. In our sublime and superior common sense such a law appears trivial. Yet if we could calculate the vast amount of money annually lost to this country by insects, caused by the wanton and wicked destruction of birds, it might not seem so very trifling after all. It might be even found to be advantageous to import or raise large quantities of insectivorous birds.

EAST SIDE—*Lower Shelf.*—Regent Oriole of Australia...Red-breasted Meadow-Lark of Chili...Black Cassican of Tierra del Fuego...Australian Shrike of New South Wales, &c.

WEST SIDE.—Cassicans, Crows, and Meadow-Larks from Brazil and Australia. The beautiful black birds at the north end are the Satin Birds.

CASE 6.

Fishes.

CASE 7.

EAST SIDE.—Humming Birds from Chili, Brazil, &c.

WEST SIDE—*Upper Shelf.*—Kingfishers from the Sandwich and Cape de Verde Islands, Australia, Malacca, Brazil, &c...Goat Suckers or Night Jars...Great Ibyan of Brazil.

The Kingfishers, of all British birds, have the most brilliant plumage. The classic name of this beautiful bird was *Halcyon,* and the phrase "Halcyon Days," as applied to times of unusual prosperity, is said to have been derived from the notion, for which there was no foundation, that the bird hatched its eggs in a floating nest, and that during its incubation there was always a calm at sea.

WEST SIDE—*Middle Shelf.*—Blue-winged Thrush...Sunbirds, representing in the Old World the Humming Birds of the American Continent.

Of this group, distinguished by their long, slender bills, and by the curious structure of their tongues, which are long, and usually divided into threads or filaments like a brush, it has been remarked that it is among the most interesting of the animal world. Among those in the case may be enumerated the Hoopoes and Sunbirds, the males of which have beautiful plumage, and sing agreeably; they are most common in the warm regions of the Eastern Hemisphere; the Honey-Eaters of Australia, whose tongue is terminated by a bunch of delicate filaments, admirably adapted for licking up the sugared sweets of the flower-cups; and the Creepers, Nut-hatchers, Wrens, and other small birds that feed on insects, chiefly obtained by striking the bark of trees. But far the most interesting of the *tenuirostres* are the exquisite little Humming Birds.

EAST SIDE.—Megalophus of Brazil, very curious....Fly Catchers...Bird of Paradise.... the Rifle Bird, &c.

Lower Shelf.—Thrushes and Wrens from all parts of the world....Red Toucan of Brazil, very rare...Green and Blue Tanagers.

CASE 8.

Fishes.

CASE 9.

Parrots, inhabitants of all parts of the world except Europe....Parroquets, Cockatoos, (large white birds;) Aracans, Toucans, Cuckoos, from New South Wales and Brazil principally....The Funereal Cockatoo is dressed in mourning suit. The Woodpecker of Brazil, on the middle shelf, west side, is worthy of notice, also the Toucans and Aracans. On the lower shelf are Trogons...Tamatia...Barbets, or Puff Birds.

CASE 10.

Fishes, mainly collected by Pacific Railroad and Mexican Boundary Expeditions.

CASE 11.

Kites...Hawks...Buzzards....Falcons, the most courageous in proportion to their size of all birds of prey.

The most remarkable is the Peregrine Falcon, formerly used in the sport of hawking. These falcons were very expensive; the use of them was permitted only to persons of rank, and to injure one of their nests, even on one's own grounds, was a crime severely punishable. Their power of wing is almost incredible. A case is recorded of a falcon flying 1,350 miles in 24 hours, or nearly sixty miles an hour. When flown at a heron or any other bird, their plan was to chase the bird, mount above it, and then swoop down upon it. To do this in a proper manner they required training.

The beautiful birds at the north end with long tails are the Peacock Trogons. At the same end, east side, is the Caracara Eagle. On the lower shelf are Owls from Australia, Brazil, &c. The one with wings extended, is from Malacca.

CASE 12.

Fishes.

Table Case, between Cases 11 *and* 13, is filled with Eggs of Eagles, Hawks, Owls, Woodpeckers, Cuckoos, &c.

CASE 13.

Fishes. Observe the singular Hippocampus, or Sea-Horse, from Old Point Comfort, Va. Also the same from California.

At the EAST END OF THE HALL we see two cases containing Birds and Animals, mounted by the skilful taxidermist, J. G. Bell, of N. Y., and exhibited by him at the World's Fair, as specimens of his art.

The DOOR leads to the taxidermist's or preparation room, where Mr. C. Drexler is engaged in mounting animals for the Smithsonian Museum. Any persons having a pet bird or animal which they desire to preserve, can have it beautifully mounted by Mr. Drexler, at a moderate charge.

Ball struck by lightning.

This ball was attached to the top of a lantern placed on the top of the old dome of the Capitol, in which it was proposed to use the Drummond light for illuminating the city. The experiment failed, and a stroke of lightning left its mark on this ball, which is here exhibited.

Cinnabar or Vermilion, the ore from which mercury or quicksilver is obtained.

This specimen, from California, weighs 400 pounds, is very rich in mercury, and was exhibited in the World's Fair as a sample of the mineral wealth of the Pacific State. The mines of Almaden, in Spain, are the most celebrated. Mercury boils at 670° and becomes solid at 40° below zero.

CASE 14.

We have here a great collection of Rattlesnakes. Every species may be seen, and from all parts of the country.

It was proposed, in the early days of our history, to adopt the rattlesnake as our national emblem, but the eagle was selected in preference.

Window between Cases 14 *and* 15.—Specimens of American Woods.

Table Case.—Specimens of Palæontology, or fossil remains of plants and animals dug out of the earth.

These singular and interesting fossils are from Nebraska, a district called "Mauvaises Terres" or Bad Lands. The valley is 90 miles in length and 30 in breadth. Its most depressed portion is 300 feet below the general level of the surrounding country. All over the surface thousands of abrupt, irregular, prismatic, and columnar masses are standing, extending to a height of one or two hundred feet. It resembles a large city. It is an immense cemetery of extinct animals, the bottom of what was once an extensive lake. The specimens are Mammalia, and Chelonia or Turtles. There are two remarkable species of Rhinoceros differing from any remains of this animal found in other parts of the globe. These are the first discovered in America. A full description of these fossils has been written by Dr. Jos. Leidy, of Philadelphia, and published in the Smithsonian Contributions to Knowledge.

CASE 15.

Serpents.

CASE 16.

EAST SIDE—*Upper Shelf.*—The most prominent object is (No. 43) the Bald Eagle or White-headed Eagle. It has its wings extended.

Benjamin Franklin thus speaks:—"For my part, I wish the Bald Eagle had not been chosen as the representative of our country. He is a bird of bad moral character; he does not get his living honestly. You may have seen him perched on some dead tree, where, too lazy to fish for himself, he watches the labors of the Fishing Hawk; and when that diligent bird has at length taken a fish, and is bearing it to his nest for the support of its mate and young ones, the Bald Eagle pursues him and takes it from him. With all this injustice, he is never in good case, but like those among men who live by sharping and robbing, he is generally poor. Besides he is a rank coward; the little King-Bird, not bigger than a Sparrow, attacks him boldly, and drives him out of the district. He is therefore by no means a proper emblem for the brave and honest Cincinnati of America, who have driven all the King-Birds from our country."

Next in order are Duck Hawks...Black-capped Hawks...Prairie Falcons...Pigeon Hawks... Sparrow Hawks.

The Sparrow Hawk was in high estimation among the Egyptians; and their god Osiris was worshipped under this name.

Middle Shelf.—No. 39, The Golden Eagle, or the Ring-tailed Eagle.

The Golden Eagle is held by the American Indians, as it is by almost every other people, to be an emblem of might and courage; and the young Indian warrior glories in his eagle plume as the most honorable ornament with which he can adorn himself. A warrior will exchange a valuable horse for the tail-feathers of a single eagle.

Swainson's Hawk...Brown, Baird's, Red-shouldered, Red-bellied, Broad-winged Hawks.

Lower Shelf.—OWLS, rapacious nocturnal birds, inhabiting all parts of the world except Australia. There are specimens of the Barn, Prairie, Burrowing, Pigmy, Short-eared, Long-eared, Saw-whet, Snowy, Great Horned, Mottled, Great Gray, Barred, Sparrow, and other Owls.

The Burrowing Owl is the constant companion of the Prairie Dog, (see case 30,) and lives in perfect harmony with him in his underground quarters.

"Looking at some of these wise-looking birds, with their big round heads, docked bodies, and goggle eyes, one could almost believe the story of the cockney sportsman, who, having shot something that he saw flying overhead, as he and a companion were passing through a churchyard in the evening, cried out in horror as he picked it up fluttering beside a tombstone, "Oh, Jack, I have shot a cherub!"

CASE 16.

WEST SIDE—*Upper Shelf.*—Blue-backed, Sharp-shinned, and other Hawks....The Bald Eagle.

Middle Shelf.—American Bald Eagle...Western Red-tailed Hawk, the most abundant species west of the Rocky mountains...Rough-legged Hawk...Black, Marsh, and Sparrow Hawks...The Golden Eagle, very rare. This bird preys on lambs, fawns, &c.

Lower Shelf.—Turkey Buzzard...Mexican, White-tailed, Swallow-tailed, Marsh, Fish, and other Hawks...Mississippi Kite...Black Kite...Gray Sea Eagle...Northern Sea Eagle... the California Vulture, the largest species in Western United States.

Four of these Vultures were seen to drag off the body of a grizzly bear weighing 200 pounds, a distance of six hundred feet. It is inferior in size only to the gigantic Condor of South America.

CASE 17.

Serpents.

CASE 18.

East Side—*Upper Shelf.*—Red and yellow-shafted Flickers...Chuck-Will's-Widow... Whip-poor-will...Wood, and other Pewees...Olive-sided and other Fly-Catchers, which catch their insect prey flying...King Birds.

The Scissor-tail or Swallow-tailed Fly-Catcher or the Texas Bird of Paradise, is an exquisitely beautiful and graceful bird,

Middle Shelf.—Swallows...Thrushes...Warblers...Stone Chat, &c.

Lower Shelf.—Finches...Sparrows...Cross-bills...Oregon Snow-Bird...Buntings.

West Side—*Upper Shelf.*—Cuckoos...Woodpeckers...Sapsuckers...Humming Birds.

The feathers of the Red-shafted Woodpecker are highly prized by the Indians on account of their beauty and rarity. They ornament their head dresses with them.

Middle Shelf.—Warblers...Red Birds...Tanagers. Notice especially the California Ant-eating Woodpecker.

Found in every portion of the country. They are very gay and sociable, and make a great deal of noise. In the fall this species has the curious and peculiar habit of laying up provisions against the inclement season. Small round holes are dug in the bark of the pine and oak, into each one of which is inserted an acorn, and so tightly is it fitted or driven in that it is with difficulty extracted. The bark of the pine trees, when thus filled, presents at a short distance the appearance of being studded with brass headed nails. Stowed away in large quantities in this manner, the acorns not only supply the wants of the Woodpeckers, but the Squirrels, Mice, and Jays avail themselves likewise of the fruits of its provident labor. The nest is hollowed out from the body of a tree or some decayed branch, and varies from 6 inches to 2 feet in depth. The eggs, 4 or 5 in number, of a pure white, are placed at the bottom of this cavity, resting on the soft bed of dust and chips which have there fallen during the labor of excavation.

Lower Shelf.—Nut-hatchers...Titmice...Wrens...Shrikes, or Butcher-Birds.

They derive their name from the manner in which they treat the insects, young frogs, &c., on which they feed, often impaling them on thorns, and tearing them to pieces at their leisure.

Sky-larks...Grosbeaks...Finches...Creepers.

CASE 19.

Serpents.

CASE 20.

East Side—*Upper Shelf.*—Cardinal Grosbeaks.

The Cardinal Grosbeak is also called the "Red Bird" and the "Virginia Nightingale." With the most brilliant plumage, it unites the sweetest song.

Middle Shelf.—Partridges...Prairie Hens...Ptarmigans.

Large numbers of Ptarmigan are sent from Norway to London every winter. The birds are caught in snares, and kept in a frozen state for the dealers. One dealer will buy and sell 50,000 Ptarmigans in a season.

Lower Shelf.—Golden Plovers, or Bull-heads...King Plover...Piping Plover...The largest is the Black-bellied.

These birds prefer bare places, repose on the ground, and never perch at night or roost on trees. Inhabits the entire American continent.

Kill-deer, one of the few birds of our country known to all classes and ages of the people.

West Side—*Upper Shelf.*—Jays...Crows...Ravens.

The Raven is the largest bird of the crow kind. It is found in all climes, and its age is said at times to reach one hundred years. It sustains equally the warmth of the sun at the equator and the cold of Iceland; it feeds on everything, and is highly venerated in some countries.

Orioles...Arctic Blue Bird.

Middle Shelf.—Cock of the Plains, or Sage Cock...Oregon Cocks...Grouse.

Lower Shelf.—Snipes...Buff-breasted Sandpiper, a little bird of remarkable and handsome plumage...Marbled Godwit, a great favorite with sportsmen for shooting...Long-billed Curlew, abundant in every part of the United States.

CASE 21.

Reptiles...Notice the Mexican Horned Frog.

This curious animal will live for months without food. Quite recently there were two live specimens received at the Smithsonian Institution, in a letter from Huntsville, Texas. When taken out of the envelope, they appeared flattened and lifeless, but a few moments in the fresh air made them very lively, and they can now be seen in the taxidermist's room.

CASE 22.

EAST SIDE.—*Upper Shelf.*—Sea Ducks.

Middle Shelf.—River Ducks...Mallard, or Green Head...Black Duck, the largest, and finest for eating...Pintail, Sprigtail, English, Blue-winged, Green-winged, Red-breasted Teals...Sora...Common Rail, or Ortolan.

The most abundant and most universally known bird of its genus, inhabiting the United States, and everywhere known as the "Rail." The specimens from California are precisely identical with others from the banks of the Delaware river.

Lower Shelf.—Wild Turkeys...Mexican Turkeys.

Among the most beautiful of known birds. The feathers exhibit reflections of metallic bronze, gold, green, and blue.

WEST SIDE—*Upper Shelf.*—Shoveller...Spoon-bill.....Bald-pate....American and English Widgeons.

Middle Shelf.—Teals.

Lower Shelf.—White Crane...Whooping Crane.

The White Crane is one of the rarest birds to be found in collections.

Sand-hill or Brown Crane, or Stork, from California.

In the early settlement of that country, one of these cranes sold from $16 to $18 in the San Francisco market, to take the place of the turkey at the Christmas dinner.

CASE 23.

Frogs.

Here are also the Hyla, or Tree-Frogs, which have the power of walking on polished surfaces, and of attaching themselves by their feet to, and walking with their bodies suspended on the under side of, the smoothest leaves.

CASE 24.

EAST SIDE—*Upper Shelf.*—The Gulls...The Laughing Gull...Franklin's Rosy Gull.... Hooded, Bonaparte's, Kittiwake, and Yellow-billed Gulls.

The most beautiful are known by the dark-colored hood or cowl which envelopes the head in summer.

Middle Shelf.—Fishing Ducks...Goosander...Sheldrake, or Fish Ducks...Red-breasted Merganser...Smew.

Lower Shelf.—American Geese...Canada Goose...Hutchins' Goose...Brant.

WEST SIDE—*Upper Shelf.*—The Terns...Marsh, Caspian, Royal, Elegant, Cabot's, Havell's, Sooty, Arctic, Roseate, and other Terns.

Mostly found on the sea-coast and bays, are much on the wing, and are remarkable for their easy and buoyant flight.

The Frigate Pelican, or Man-of-War Bird.

Its power of flight is not excelled by any other bird. Very tyrannical.

Middle Shelf.—Fishing Ducks.

Lower Shelf.—Rough-billed and Brown Pelicans. The American Swan, equally abundant on all parts of the continent. The young bird is brown....Trumpeter Swan, very large and powerful...Cormorants.

PELICAN.—"In the Gulf of California, a small black gull follows the pelican incessantly on its flight, and as the latter plunged into the sea after fish, the gull would immediately alight by its side. The pelican, emerging from the water to discharge the fluid collected in the gular sac, would drop its bill, when the fish partially protruding from between its mandibles, the gull would seize upon one and drag it out, as his share of the booty. Although this feat is of hourly occurrence, the pelican never offers the least resistance, or shows any anger or impatience at the intrusion or impudence of his little neighbor, who, like a tax-gatherer, follows him through life, an evil inevitable."

CASE 25.

Frogs.

CASE 26.

This case contains a number of interesting specimens. No. 67, Alligator from Florida... 68, Sea-cow from the Amazon river...69, 70, 71, 75, 79, Sea-Leopards, or Seals.

The brain of the seal is well-developed, and the degree of sagacity and attachment shown in domestication—for

they are very easily tamed, and taught to perform tricks—is evidence of superior intelligence. Cuvier tells of a seal who would raise himself erect, and take a staff in his flippers, like a sentinel. At the word of command, he would lie down on his right side or his left, according to order, or tumble head over heels. He gave a paw when requested, like a dog, and protruded his lips for a kiss.
The Roman Emperor Augustus always carried the skin of a sea-leopard as a protection against lightning.

Nos. 72, 73, 76, Albatrosses, the largest sea-birds known.

They will swallow a salmon of 4 or 5 pounds weight. They never attack other sea-birds.
"If the Eagle is called the king of birds, the Albatross ought to be called the queen, so queen-like and stately is her course on the wing, and so dignified, mild, and unfearing is her expression when captured. When on the wing it is the very beau-ideal of beauty and grace. This glorious bird is the most beautiful and lovable object of the animate world which the adventurer meets with in all the South Pacific."—*Rev. H. T. Cheever.*

No. 74, Saw-fish...No. 78, Skull of a Sea Leopard...No. 80, American Beaver, a splendid specimen of this interesting animal, whose habits and history are familiar to all....No. 81 is a part of a tree cut by the Beaver...No. 82, Porpoise or Sea Hog.

Porpoises swim in shoals and drive the mackerel, herrings, and salmon before them, pursuing them up the bays, with the same eagerness as a pack of dogs after a hare. In some places they almost darken the sea as they rise above water to take breath. In fine weather they leap, roll, and tumble about in the most sportive manner. The oil procured from the fat surrounding the body of the Porpoise is of the purest kind, and the skin, when tanned and dressed, is used for wearing apparel, and for coverings for carriages. As an article of food, the flesh is highly esteemed. It is the great dainty of the Greenlanders, and he quaffs its oil as the most delicious of draughts.

The large fish near the east side of the case is a STURGEON, and the one near it, with the fin on its back, is a SHARK, both caught in the Potomac river.

CENTRE OF THE HALL, EAST END.

Case of specimens of Silver, Lead, and Copper Ores, from the mines of the Sonora Exploring and Mining Company, Tubac, Gadsden's Purchase, New Mexico...Specimens from the mines of New Granada...Gold, Silver, Galena, &c., from various parts of the world.

Raised Model, representing the Geology of Switzerland.

The large case contains a magnificent and unique collection of Birds' Nests and Eggs... Notice especially in the upper part, the Oriole Nests...Marsh Wren Nests...The green eggs of the Catbird...Eggs of Chuck-Will's-Widow....Humming Birds' Nests, very rare and valuable. These nests readily bring a high price at any time....Night Hawk's Eggs....In the lower part, the Pelican Nest and Eggs...Loon Eggs...Alligator and Ostrich Eggs...The largest egg is that of the Giant Fossil Bird, of Madagascar.

Though probably extinct, the species may be in existence in the unknown interior of the Island, as is believed by the natives. This egg is 12½ inches long by 8½ inches wide, the shell one-tenth of an inch thick.

Notice in this part of the hall the Meteorite described on page 23 of this volume.

Next visit the WEST END OF THE HALL, and commence on the south side at—

CASE 28.

No. 1, Wolverine or Glutton, from Salt Lake, very fierce and cunning...No. 2, Jaguar, or American Tiger.

The following narrative shows the character of this animal: "In 1825, near Santa Fe, N. M., a lay brother, after having made confession and concluded his prayers, entered the sacristy. There he was terror-stricken on opening the door and seeing himself face to face with a Jaguar. In a moment the poor man was in the clutches of the beast, which dragged its victim into a back corner to finish the bloody work. The guardian of the convent hearing the noise hurried to the room, and had scarcely become aware of what had happened when the animal leaped upon his second victim and despatched him. After a while several other men attempted to open the bloody sacristy, but not without meeting a similar fate, for the first one opening the door was immediately slain. After he had killed four victims, the roaring of the Jaguar attracted the people of the convent, and by boring a hole in the door they finally succeeded in shooting the dreadful monster. The convent where this occurred is on the banks of the Rio Bravo, which, after freshets, overflows the islands in front of the town, and all the animals living in the thickets are driven up. This animal entered the garden of the convent, and thence, by a small door accidentally left open, the sacristy."

No. 3, Three American Wild Cats, from the Sonorian Mountains near Fort Yuma...4, Young Black Bear, from Warsaw, Illinois...5, Red Wild Cat, from Washington Territory... 6, Canada Lynx, from Medicine Bow Creek, near Fort Laramie...7, Grizzly Bear, from Medicine Bow Creek, near Fort Laramie...8, Skin of Bush Goat, of Africa...9, Skin of Red Buck Deer, of Africa...10, Black Orang-Outang, of Africa, female...11, Skull, hand, and foot of the Chimpanzee, of Africa...12, Rope made from grass on the Gold Coast of Africa... 13, Sankywin Monkey, from Demarara, Guiana...14, Hooraway Monkey, from Demarara, Guiana...15, Ground Monkey...16, Ring-tail Monkey...17, Ground Monkey.

CASE 29.

Fishes from the China seas.

CASE 30.

EAST SIDE—*Upper Shelf.*—Bats, from New South Wales, &c...Sloth, from British Guiana, rare...Gophers, of California, etc., very destructive to the products of the farm and garden... Salamanders...Prairie Dogs.

These are almost the only inhabitants of the high, dry prairie land destitute of every form of vegetation except grass. A Prairie Dog, however, is always fat. They are known to all western travelers, and found in immense numbers on the overland route to California.

Middle Shelf.—Common Mink, the pest of farmers—one has been known to kill 30 chickens in a night. Weasels...Pine Martens, or American Sable.

The Ornithorynchus Paradoxus, or Duck Bill.

This is an extraordinary animal, and when it was first described, and even after its skin was received in England, naturalists hesitated to believe in its existence. It is a native of Australia, where it is called Water-mole. It lives almost entirely in the water.

Lower Shelf.—Raccoons....Opossums....Skunks....Wood-Chucks....Ground Hogs....Musk Rats, found over the whole country.

WEST SIDE—*Upper Shelf.*—Bats.

Middle Shelf.—Musk-Rats...Weasels...Armadillos.

The Armadillo is gifted with extraordinary strength—sometimes elevating a weight placed on his back of an 100 pounds. It rolls itself up like a ball, and sleeps nearly all day. It is much sought for as food. It is inoffensive, and can be handled with impunity. Armadillos never attempt to bite, nor has nature given them any other means of defence than the ease and rapidity with which they avoid danger by burrowing. Their food consists of fallen fruits, roots, and worms; but they do not reject carrion, and have been known to penetrate into human graves.

Lower Shelf.—Bassaris Astuta, Civet Cat.

Called Squirrel Cat by Texans. Lives among rocks and trees. It is easily tamed, and makes a mild and playful pet. It is something between fox and raccoon—sole representative in the New World of the genets, civets, ichneumons, &c., of the Old.

CASE 31.

Toads.

Window Case.—Woods collected by Exploring Expedition.

CASE 32.

Upper Shelf.....Squirrels of various kinds.

Middle Shelf.—Hares...Rabbits...Prairie Dogs...Mice...Moles...Rats.

Lower Shelf.—Badgers...Ground Hogs...Beaver.

The Agouti of the West Indies is the largest quadruped indigenous to these islands. They live exclusively on vegetables.

Hoary Marmots...Wood Chucks...Civet Cats, &c.

CASE 33.

Star-fishes.

Window Case.—Plaster Casts or Medallions.

CASE 34.

Corals.

This is one of the most complete and beautiful collections extant, and has been arranged by Prof. J. D. Dana, of Yale College.

Middle Shelf.—Crystals of Sulphur, Feldspar, and Lava, from the craters on the Sandwich Islands, collected by the Exploring Expedition.

In procuring these specimens there was great risk. The persons walked over a crust of only two or three inches of black lava, beneath which was a mass which lighted a pole instantaneously when pierced through it.

CASE 35.

Sepia, or Cuttle-Fish...Nautilus, and other Mollusks.

Window Case.—Woods.

CASE 36.

Corals.

Every branch of Coral may be considered as a tree or plant, all the buds of which are animated polypes.

Sponges.

As to the true nature of these extraordinary substances, naturalists are not altogether agreed. They are usually placed in the animal kingdom, and erected into a distinct class of radiata, called *Porifera*, analogous in some respects to the zoophyta. What is seen here is, however, only the skeleton of the living being, which is but a thin gelatinous substance.

CASE 37.

Palæmons...Prawns or Shrimps...Galatheidæ, a group of Crustaceans.

Window Case.—Woods.

CASE 38.

Corals and Sponges....Notice the Sea Mushroom.

It has a beautiful stony cell, consisting of a thick round plate several inches in diameter, with numerous thin vertical plates rising from it, and radiating from its centre.

The Brain-stone, so called from its resemblance to the human brain.

Some of the coral reefs are known to be one thousand miles long and more than three hundred broad.

CASE 39.

Crustacea...Dromidiæ, &c.

CASE 40.

Crustacea...Ocypodes, &c.

NORTH SIDE OF THE HALL.

CASE 41.

Fishes...Abranchiates, &c.

CASE 42.

Crabs.

Window Case.—Plaster cast of Old Sarum, Wiltshire, England....Relics from Nicaragua.

The small figure representing an animal couchant was regarded with great veneration by the Indians. See page 19.

CASE 43.

Exotic Birds.

CASE 44.

Fishes, Bonaparte Collection.

Window Case.—Stone Sphynx from Egypt, presented to E. DeLeon, Consul General of the U. S., by the British Consul General.

CASE 45.

Wild Muscovy Duck...Black-winged Goose of Chili...Sandwich Island Goose...Loggerhead, Antarctic, Upland, Bustard Geese...Black Swan of Australia...Penguins...King Penguin—is a great thief.

They occupy the same place in the southern hemisphere that the Auks do in the northern.

Penguins are said to unite in themselves the qualities of men, fowls, and fishes. Like men, they are upright; like fowls, they are feathered; and like fish, they have fin-like instruments that beat the water before, and serve for all the purposes of swimming. From 30 to 40,000 Penguins have been seen at a time. They are arranged when on shore in as compact a manner and in as regular ranks as a regiment of soldiers, and are classed with the greatest order, the younger birds being in one situation, moulting birds in another, setting hens in a third, and so on. They will stand still and be knocked down without making any effort to escape.

Kiwi-kiwi.

It is much like the Penguin. Whilst at rest it has the singular habit of resting on the top of its bill, which is its most characteristic position. The natives hunt it for its skin for dresses.

Window Case.—Woods.

CASE 46.

Fishes.

CASE 47.

Exotic Birds...Ducks...Gannetts...Booby...Frigate Pelican, or Man-of-War Bird.

The Booby is so stupid that he will sit still and be knocked on the head on the shore or a ship. They are much persecuted by the Man-of-War Bird.

CASE 48.

Fishes, Paraguay Expedition.

CASE 49.

Birds from Sandwich Islands, Tierra del Fuego, Chili, &c...The Oyster-Catcher...Noddy... Wandering Albatross...Stormy Petrels, or Mother Carey's Chickens.

CASE 50.

Serpents and Reptiles.

CASE 51.

The Ibis.

The red bird is the Scarlet Ibis, worshipped by the Egyptians, one of the most celebrated birds of antiquity.

New Holland Crane...Brazilian Cranes...Tookaroo, a rare species of Crane.

CASE 52.

Reptiles from Brazil, and from the Paris Museum.

Between Cases 52 *and* 53.—The identical dress worn by Dr. E. K. KANE, the celebrated American Arctic Explorer, and brought by him to this Museum. We quote the following from the account of his travels :

"The clothing or personal outfit demands the nicest study of experience. Rightly clad, he is a lump of deformity, waddling over the ice, unpicturesque, uncouth, and seemingly helpless. The fox-skin jumper, or *kapetah*, is a closed shirt, fitting very loosely to the person, but adapted to the head and neck by an almost air-tight hood, the *nessak*. Underneath the *kapetah* is a similar garment, but destitute of the hood, which is a shirt. It is made of bird skins, chewed in the mouth by the women until they are perfectly soft, and it is worn with this unequalled down next the body. More than 500 *auks* have been known to contribute to a garment of this description. The lower extremities are guarded by a pair of bear-skin breeches, the *nannooke*. The foot gear consists of a bird-skin sock, with a padding of grass over the sole. Outside of this is a bear-skin leg.

In this dress, a man will sleep upon his sledge with the atmosphere at 93° below our freezing point. The only additional articles of dress are, a fox's tail held between the teeth to protect the nose in a wind, and mitts of seal-skin well wadded with sledge straw."

Dr. Kane, however, had to add to the dress described "furs and woolens, layer upon layer, inside, like the shards of an artichoke, till he was rounded into absolute obesity."

CASE 53.

No. 18, Big Horn, or Mountain Sheep.

Found on rocky sierras and other places where the want of water forbids the existence of every other ruminant.

No. 19, Mountain Sheep, from Fort Tejon, Cal...No. 20, Kangaroo, U. S. Exploring Expedition...No. 21, Guanaco or Llama—a young one of No. 25...No. 22, Virginia Deer, from Medicine Bow...No. 23, Black-tailed Deer, from California...No. 24, Black-tailed Deer, from Oregon...No. 25, Guanaco or Llama...No. 26, Black-tailed Deer, from California...No. 27, Prong-horn Antelope, from Yellowstone River...No. 28, A young Elk...Nos. 29 and 30, Virginia Deer...No. 31, Patagonia Deer...Nos. 32, 33, 34, 35, Musk Deer, from New Holland... No. 36, Kangaroo...No. 37, Antelope, from Cape of Good Hope...Nos. 38, 39, 40, Musk Deer.

CASE 54.

Serpents and Reptiles from South America, Central America, and the North Pacific.

Next examine the large table case in the middle of the west end of the room, in which is a fine collection of Sea-eggs and Star-fishes. Notice particularly the specimens at the east end with their curious teeth...Echinidæ, or Sea Urchins or Sea Eggs.

These are found generally on sandy shores, and prefer quiet and secluded pools. Some make excavations in solid rock. Their food consists of sea-weeds and small crustaceæ.

The Star-fishes.

Their structure is that of a number of tough, leathery rays diverging from a central disk. In this disk is the mouth, which opens into a stomach filling the disk and branching off into the rays. The various forms are innumerable. They are found in every climate.

The most interesting, however, are the comatula, or sea-wigs. They have a branch-like structure, like that of a gorgon's head; but what makes them peculiarly interesting is, that they are the recent representatives of a tribe of sea-animals now all but extinct, although found in immense abundance in a fossil state. These curious animals of a former era are called crinoideæ, and they were so numerous that Prof. Forbes says the remains of their skeletons constitute great tracts of the dry land as it now appears.

The structure of the shell of the echinus, which consists of a number of pentagonal pieces fitting together, the method by which it is increased by a calcareous secretion from the body of the animal, and the mechanism by which the spines are attached, are subjects of great admiration among naturalists. The interior structure is very simple, consisting only of a powerful and muscular mouth armed with strong teeth, and of an intestinal tube wound twice round the inside of the shell.

All are not of a globular shape. Some are so depressed as to be popularly known as Sea-Pancakes.

Lizard-tailed Star-fishes, or Brittle Stars.

In the lower part of the case are fine specimens of Turtles.

They have the faculty of falling to pieces, or at least of throwing off the ends of their rays when siezed or otherwise alarmed.

UPPER GALLERIES.

EAST END, NORTH SIDE.—Geological and Mineralogical collections, not yet arranged for public exhibition.

CASE 63.

SOUTH SIDE.—Human Skulls from the Feejee Islands, New Zealand, California, Mexico, North American Indians, &c. One of the Skulls is of Vendovi, the Feejee Chief and Murderer.

There are 150 skulls in this case, which is one of the most interesting in the collection, and calculated to excite feelings very different from those experienced in examining any other specimens.

Window Case.—Skull of an Elephant.

The other cases in this gallery are devoted to Skulls and Skeletons. They are not arranged for exhibition.

The large mounted skeletons in the windows are those of the Ostrich and the Lama.

WEST GALLERY—SOUTH SIDE.

One of the most extensive and curious ethnological collections in the world. Passing to the eastern extremity of the gallery commence at—

CASE 70.

Specimens from the North American Indians, including Head Dresses....Canoes.... Feather Blankets.....Water-Baskets.....Indian Cradles.....Water-Bottles of the Utahs..... Indian Pillow, stuffed with Buffalo hair...Bows and Arrows...Pipes, &c., &c.

Among the most interesting articles are specimens of the Calumets or Pipes of Peace, and the Wampum Belts. The bowls of these pipes are always made of one particular kind of stone of a cherry red color, brought from a quarry which the Indians believe consists of a huge army of Red Men whom the Great Spirit turned at once into stone. The shaft is usually young ash. Wampum is the Indian name for ornaments manufactured by the Indians of parti-colored shells, which they get on the shores of fresh-water streams, and file and cut into bits of half an inch in length, and perforate, giving to them the shape of pieces of broken pipe stems, string on deer sinews and wear on their necks, or weave ingeniously into war belts. Wampum was used as a circulating medium instead of coin.

CASE 71.

Collections made by the U. S. Exploring Expedition in the Feejee Islands...Cannibal Cooking Pots.

The Feejees are Cannibals. The flesh of women is preferred to that of men, and that part of the arm above the elbow and the thigh are regarded as the choicest parts. So highly do they esteem this food, that the greatest praise they can bestow on a delicacy is to say that it is as tender as a dead man.

Vessel for mixing oil...Fishing Nets of twine, from the bark of the Hibiscus...Flute of Bamboo, and other musical instruments...Paddles...Mask and Wig worn in dances...War Conch, blown as the sign of hostilities...Fishing Spears...War Clubs...Feejee Wigs.

The usual sign of mourning is to crop the hair, and as they are very vain, and the hair takes a long time to grow again, they use a wig as a substitute.

Native Cloth, worn as a turban on the head.

None but Chiefs are allowed to wear this. The more the hair is distended, the greater is their pride. Barbers are very important personages, and are employed on all occasions.

Between Cases 71 and 72.—Feejee Spears...Feejee Drum.

Made of a hollow trunk of a tree. It is sounded by beating on the inner side with a mallet. It is said its sound may be heard from seven to ten miles.

CASE 72.

Feejee Islands.—Likus, or Petticoat worn by the Feejee Women...Sunshades, made of a

single Palm-leaf...Pillow of Wood...Basket...Shell Ornaments, made of Trochus Shell...
Armlets...Necklaces...Headbands of Feathers...Baskets...Fans of Cocoa-nut leaves...Native
Cloth, from bark of Paper Mulberry...Floor Mat, from the leaves of the Pandanus...Neck-
lace of human teeth...Fish Vertebræ...Braided Cord of the husk of the Cocoa-nut...Feejee
Oracle, kept in the Temple and consulted by the Priests.

This Oracle is generally covered with scarlet and white seeds stuck on with gum. It is hollow, has an ear on
one side, and a mouth and nose on the other.

The figure like an idol, with a wooden plate at the top and hooks at the feet, is a contri-
vance used by the Feejees to save provisions from the attacks of the Feejee rat, which is a
great pest...Sea-slug, or Biche de Mer, a great article of trade...Model of Canoe, showing
the peculiar style of construction with the outrigger....Hair combs, pins, &c.

The mode of wearing the comb is an indication of rank. None but the king wears it in front. The lower orders
wear it behind the ear.

Whale's tooth...Female Dress.

The usual price of a wife is a whale's tooth, and this once paid, the husband has the entire right to the person
of the wife, whom he may even kill and eat if he feels so disposed.

The women's dress is quite becoming and graceful. It is a kind of fringe made of cocoa-nut leaves, cut into
slips about a foot long, and tied by one end to a string, which goes around the middle, It has a light and
elegant appearance, and yields to any portion of the body, yet never becomes entangled or out of order.

CASE 73.

Samoan or Navigator Islands.—Specimens of Tapa, or native cloth.

The tapa is often printed in colors. The natives form tablets of pieces of large cocoa-nut leaves. One side of
the tablet is kept smooth and even, and upon this cocoa-nut fibres are sewed, so as to form the required pattern
which is, of course, raised upon the surface of the tablet. These tablets are wet with a piece of cloth well soaked
in the dye, after which the tapa, which for this purpose is well bleached and beautifully white, is laid upon them
and pressed into close contact. The dye is made from herbs and roots, and is of various colors.

Fishing Nets...War Clubs...Shell-bead Necklaces...Flute...War Conchs...Fans...Baskets...
Pillows of Bamboo...Paddles...Spears made of iron wood, pointed with the sting of the ray-
fish, which, on breaking off in the body, causes certain death...Bows and Arrows used for
catching Lupi, or Pigeons.

Much time is devoted to capturing and taming these birds, which may be seen in almost every house, and even
in their canoes, where perches are erected expressly for them.

Mats.

Among the mats are some of as fine texture and as soft as if made of cotton. These are solely possessed by
the chiefs, and are considered as their choicest treasures, and are so much coveted that wars have been made to
obtain possession of them.

CASE 74.

Sandwich Islands.—Tonga or Friendly islands.—Pieces of the rock on which Capt. Cook,
the celebrated navigator, was killed...Adzes of Cassus Shell...War Clubs...Native Cloth...
Pestles for pounding Kalo...Quoits...Fans...Raw Cotton, raised in Hawaii...Shells and Feathers worn as ornaments...Fishing-lines and Hooks...Gourd Shells...Bowls in which *Ava*, the
national drink, is prepared.

The *ava* is a root of a pungent and intoxicating nature. Young girls chew it up and spit it into a wooden
bowl; afterwards a small quantity of water is added to it, the juice is strained into cups made of cocoa-nut shells,
and all drink it. No business is done in the day till the king drinks his *ava*.

Bowls from which the food called *Poi* is eaten.

Kalo is the invaluable article of food. It is the bread of the Islanders. When made into *poi*, it is the national
dish. The kalo is cooked, then pounded up, water added, and a paste formed, which is allowed to ferment, and
is eaten with one or two fingers, according to its consistency.

Native Pelava, from human hair, and sea-horse tooth, a neck ornament...Combs...Feather
Cape worn on public occasions by King Kamehameha when a youth. Presented by him to
Com. Bolton in 1839.

The birds "Oo," from which these splendid feathers were taken, have but two feathers of the kind, one under
each wing. It is a very rare species, peculiar only to the higher regions of Hawaii, and is caught with great care
and much toil. Five of these feathers were valued at $1.50. It is computed that a million dollars were expended
on the manufacture of a cloak like this for Kamehameha. The bunches of feathers are still received in payment
of a tax to the king. They are afterwards made up into head-bands for the ladies, but few can afford to wear
them. Mantles of these feathers are not now to be seen, the cost and labor of procuring them being so great.
Specimens of these birds can be seen in Case 5.

Feather Staff, an ensign of rank...Wooden Dishes of curious forms...Canoes...Combs...
Cinctures, the dress worn by women of Tongatabu.

CASE 75.

Kingsmill, Marquesas, and Washington Islands.—These are included in what is known as Micronesia.—Native Ropes from the bark of the Cocoa-nut...Wooden, Pearl, and other Fish-hooks...Breast Plate...Shell Adzes, from Disappointment Islands...Cuirass of Rope... Beads of Wood and Shell.

Long strings of beads or braided hair are worn round the body at times a hundred fathoms in length. The hair is taken from female slaves. The beads are manufactured by the old men who are beyond doing any other labor—made of cocoa-nut and shell, ground down to a uniform size.

Ear-rings worn by the Chiefs of the Marquesas....File or Rasp of Shark's skin....A Virgin's Head-band...Wooden Dish like a boat, from Raraka...Spears...Helmet of a skin of Porcupine Fish...Images of green stone.

Around the necks of the Chiefs is hung their "HEITIKI," made of a stone of a green color, which is held very sacred, and which, with their "MEARA," a short cleaver or club, is handed down from father to son. This Heitiki has some resemblance to a human figure sitting with crossed legs.

Weapons armed with Shark's teeth...Pieces of wood worn in dances...Cap of Pandanus leaves...Mats,

Made from the leaves of the Pandanus, the yellow from the young leaves, and the brown from the old; which are prepared by beating them with a mallet to render them pliable. To the yellow mats, the greatest attention is paid. Oil impregnated with the odor of the flowers of the Pandanus, and the distilled water, are highly esteemed, both for their color and their medicinal use as stimulants.

Stilts used by Marquesas Islanders...Beautifully carved Adzes and Clubs.

CASE 76.

New Zealand.—Paddles...Spears...Blanket Mats woven by hand...Baskets...Dressing-box of a Chief...Prow of a War Canoe.

This was considered very sacred, and obtained with great difficulty. It belonged to the chief Kiwikiwi.

Shell and Wood Fish-hooks...Tinder-box...Flaxen Yarn.

The manufacture of the hemp is altogether performed by the women.

War Cloak of dog-skin, called "Topuni." This was worn by Pomare, the chief....Stone Adzes...Chisel of Tortoise Shell...Cincture and Ornament of human hair...Flute...Mats of all kinds...Bows and Arrows.

CASE 77.

Deception Island—South Shetland.—Mats, blankets, &c.

WEST GALLERY—NORTH SIDE.

CASE 78.

Egyptian Mummies.

Mummies were embalmed in Egypt in several ways, the most perfect of which was to draw the brain through the nostrils, partly with a piece of crooked iron, and partly by the infusion of drugs. They then with a knife make an incision in the side, through which they extract the intestines; these they cleanse thoroughly, washing them with palm wine, and afterwards covering them with aromatics. They then fill the body with powder of pure myrrh, cassia, and other perfumes. Having sewn up the body, it is covered with natron (a kind of soda) for the space of seventy days. It is then washed, closely wrapped in bandages of linen previously dipped in gum, and returned to the relations, who enclose it in a case of wood made to resemble a human figure. The utmost care was taken to affix marks to each mummy, by which it might be known again.

These specimens are 3,000 years old.

CASE 79.

Mummy from Oregon of a child...Peruvian Mummies, from Arica.

Believing, as they did, in immortality and the resurrection of the body, the Peruvians were very careful in burying their dead. They had a mode of embalming peculiar to themselves, which consisted of exposing the body to the intense cold of the high peaks of the mountains till it became quite dry and withered. Then, if the deceased were an Inca, he was buried with great state in his family tomb. He retained his proper apparel, and his treasures were buried w th him.

The custom of the Peruvians to bury their treasures with them, made the discovery of a tomb of some consequence to the early Spanish settlers. In 1576, a Spanish soldier, says Prescott, found in one such tomb, afterwards visited by Baron Humboldt, a mass of gold worth a million of dollars! The tombs in Central America are now being searched for golden images and treasures in the same manner.

CASE 80.

New South Wales.—Weapons...The Boomerang, a flat stick, three feet long, two inches wide, by three-fourths of an inch thick, curved or crooked in the centre, forming an obtuse angle.

This possesses the peculiar property, owing to its shape, of returning to the spot from which it was thrown, if the object aimed at was missed.

The Womerah, a throwing stick, about three feet long, with a hook at the end for throwing spears and darst, with which the Australians hit a mark 200 feet distant...Shields made of thick bark of the gum tree.

These are called hiclemara, are of a peculiar oval shape, about three feet long by six or eight inches wide, with a handle.

Curious Carved Figure from the root of a tree.

The New Zealanders have no images of worship, and no temples. The numerous grotesque images sculptured by the people are not regarded as representations of divinities. These images are often placed on the roofs of houses as decorations.

Mask worn by the South Sea Islanders.

Siamese Shirt, a net work of grass, which prevents the outer dress from touching the skin.

The Clearance of Brig Argyle, of Baltimore, at Canton, 1839—a fair specimen of a Chinese business paper...Chinese Umbrellas...Hat of Leaves...Shoes taken from the feet of a Chinese Woman, at Macao, by Dr. Wessels, 1830.

All Chinese Women pride themselves on their goat-like hoofs, and have contempt for a natural foot. It is difficult for strangers to get a sight of these deformities.

Chinese work in Stone—House, Boat, &c...Chop-sticks, used to eat food.

In China, the poorer classes eat boiled rice only, mixed with dried fish. Dogs and cats are considered delicacies above the reach of the poor. Rats, mice, and other vermin are eagerly sought after.

Chinese Fans...Compass...Japanese Crape, Silk, Cotton...Cloak of Kangaroo Skin, worn by the natives of New Holland...Cord from Kangaroo Hair....Japanese Gold and Silver Coins. The smallest coin is called *"Cash,"* in value one-twelfth of a cent...Japanese Letter and Book, said to be an interesting novel.

Reading is a favorite occupation with both sexes, and books innumerable, profusely illustrated, are printed.

Japanese Pills.

MEDICINE.—The famous *Dosia* Powder, which, when introduced into the ears, nostrils, and mouth of a rigid corpse, renders the limbs perfectly flexible.

CASE 81.

WEST SIDE.—East Indies.—Model of a Malay Prao, or armed vessel, used by the Pirates of Borneo. The Malays are mostly seamen...East Indian Arrows, poisoned with gum of the Upas...Malay Blow-Pipe, a long tube employed for projecting poisoned arrows...Arrows with Flint Heads, from Tierra del Fuego...Malay Daggers, great variety...Bows...Paddles...Shields...Spears...Coins from the East Indies...Harp from Sooloo.

EAST SIDE.—Leaf from a Brahmin's Book...Leaf from a Siamese Book...Ordinary Walking Dresses of the ladies of Lima, Peru.

However fitted this dress may be to cover intrigue, it is certainly not adapted to the display of beauty. A more awkward and absurd dress cannot well be conceived. It is by no means indicative of the wearer's rank, for frequently this disguise is ragged and tattered, and assumed, under its most forbidding aspect, to deceive or carry on an intrigue, of which it is almost an effectual cloak. In this dress it is said a wife will pass her own husband when she may be walking with her lover, and the husband may make love to his wife, without being aware it is she.

Chilian Poncho, the common Riding Cloak of the Spanish Americans...Chilian Bridles, Stirrups...Mexican Matchlock Gun...Mexican Spurs...Head-dress of Atahualpa...Earthen Ware of the ancient Peruvians—Jars, Bottles, &c.—from the Temple of Pachacamac, near Lima...Belts of Bark Cloth, from the Ascension Islands.

CASE 82.

WEST SIDE.—Siam. EAST SIDE.—Japan.—Dresses, very handsome....Gongs....Drums...Flutes...Photograph of his Majesty, PHRA BARD SONDETH PHRA PARAMENDR, MNHA MONGKUT PHRA CHOMKLAN CHAUYUHUA, the Major King of Siam and its dependencies...Swords...Daggers...Trays for fruit inlaid with Pearl.

The Japanese have the orange, lemon, fig, plum, cherry, and apricot.

Tea-service...Shears...Fans...Cloths...Silk...Loo-Choo Pipes...Cups and Saucers...Chow Chow or Refreshment Boxes...Tobacco.

The Loo-Choo islands belong to Japan. Tobacco is raised extensively, and smoking is a universal habit. Saki is an intoxicating and strong liquor, distilled from rice, which is used as a drink. At a Loo Choo dinner there are 24 courses, soup constituting eight.

Window Case.—A Chinese Plow.

The plowing is done while the fields are flooded, and is only intended for breaking up alluvial ground. It is drawn by the water ox or buffalo, the beast of burden in China.

CASE 83.

Japan.—Silks, Crapes, &c., of every variety.

The silks are equal to any in the world. The finest are made by criminals of high rank, who are confined upon a small, rocky, and unproductive island, and made to support themselves by their labor. These silks cannot be exported. All their silks and calicoes are uniformly 18 inches in width.

They have no sheep or goats, and do not make woolen fabrics.

Waiters...Small Porcelain Dolls ..Mirrors...Domestic Utensils : bowls, jars, cups, shovels, ladles...Magnificent Spears...Swords ; mountings of gold ; scabbards of shark's skin...Biche de Mer...Mats...Nails....Needles...Saws....Chisels...Planes....Agricultural Implements...Japanese Shells...Japan Printing Implements, Blocks, Ink, &c....Paper from the bark of the Mulberry, exceedingly soft and flexible, used for handkerchiefs. It endures folding, and lasts longer than ours...Models of Japanese Sanctuary, Houses, &c.

They use no glass for windows, but oiled paper or cloth.

Umbrellas made of Bamboo, and covered with a vegetable oil.

These are perfectly water proof, and can be used for a long time without injury.

All the articles of superior quality are put by the Japanese merchants into boxes of white cedar. Inferior articles are wrapped in paper.

The Japanese possess one art in which they excell the world—this is in lacquering wood work. In this operation they select the finest wood of fir or cedar to be covered with varnish which is made from the gum of the *rhus vernix*, a tree abundant in their country.

The Japanese also excell all other nations in the quality of their porcelain and swords.

They do not know how to cut or polish precious stones, but have a substitute. called *syakfdo* in which various metals are so blended and combined that they resemble fine enamel. This is used for ornamenting girdle clasps, sword hilts, boxes, &c.

CASE 84.

Amazon Expedition.—Costumes of the Savages of Ucayali river, trimmed with feathers, teeth, &c...Ants' Nest, used for spunk...Leg and Wing Bones of a Bird...Tobacco from river Madeira...Tongue of a Fish...Necklace of Berries...Minerals, Woods, Gums, &c...Bats... Lizards...Tiger Cats...Skins...Curious Brazilian Wasps' Nest, in which honey is stored up... Birds...Axes...Drums...Grass from which the Guayaquil hats are made...Sarsaparilla Roots... Blow-gun or Pucuna of the Indians.

It is made of any long, straight piece of wood, generally a species of palm. The pole is divided longitudinally ; a canal hollowed out along the centre of each part, which is well smoothed and polished ; the two parts are then fastened together with twine, and the whole covered with wax, mixed with some resin of the forest, to make it hard. A couple of boar's teeth are fitted on each side at the mouth end, and one of the curved front teeth of a small animal is placed on the top for a sight. The arrow is made of light wood—the wild cane, or the middle fibre of a species of palm leaf—which is about a foot in length, and of the thickness of an ordinary lucifer match. The end of the arrow which is placed next to the mouth is wrapped with a light, delicate sort of wild cotton, and the other end, very sharply pointed, is dipped in a vegetable poison, prepared from the juice of the creeper, mixed with strong red pepper. With this instrument the Indian will kill a small bird at thirty or forty paces. They never discharge the pucuna at a snake, for fear of the gun being made crooked like the reptile.

Hammock made of the fibres of the budding top of a species of palm.

The tree is very hard, and is defended with long, sharp thorns, so that it is a labor of a day to cut a top, split the leaves into strips of convenient breadth, and strip off the fibres, which are the outer covering of the leaves. One top usually yields about half a pound of fibres ; and when it is considered that these fibres have to be twisted, a portion of them dyed, and then woven, it will be seen that the Indian is poorly paid when he receives for a hammock 12¼ cents.

Hymeneal Bracelets.

An Indian cannot take a wife until he has passed his arms at least ten times through long stalks of the palm tree filled intentionally with large, venomous ants. When muffled in these terrible mittens, the Indian is obliged to sing and dance before every cabin.

India Rubber.

Gathered between July and January.

The tree is tall, straight, and has a smooth bark. It is sometimes eighteen inches in diameter. The milk is white and tasteless, and may be swallowed with impunity. A gash is made in the bark, and a small clay cup stuck to the tree beneath the gash. In about four hours the milk ceases to run, and each wound has given from 3 to 5 table-spoonsfull. The milk is then poured into earthen vessels and smoked. After it is prepared, it is nearly as white as milk, and gets its color from age. An industrious man can make 16 pounds of rubber a day.

CASE 85.

Monrovia, Africa.—Specimens of Negro Manufactures : Cloths, Bags, Hammocks, Paddles, Head-Dresses, Fans, Bricks, Shoes, &c...Water Jars, used by the women of Cape Palmas...Native Harp...Amulets.

CASE 86.

Unoccupied.

Attached to the iron railing, designed and manufactured expressly for this Institution at the well-known establishment of E. W. SHIPPEN, 3022 Market street, Philadelphia, which protects the upper gallery, is a splendid collection of Horns and Antlers of Elks, Deer, &c.

CATALOGUE OF WORKS OF ART.

COMMENCING AT THE SOUTHWEST CORNER OF THE ROOM.

1. PORTRAIT OF JOHN TYLER, President of the U. S., born 29th March, 1790. By Healy
2. MASSACRE OF THE INNOCENTS. Artist unknown.
3. CHRIST HEALING THE SICK. Etching by Rembrandt.
4. FULL-LENGTH PORTRAIT OF GUIZOT, Prime Minister of Louis Phillippe, a celebrated French Statesman. Painted by Healy from life.
5. PORTRAIT OF HON. WM. C. PRESTON, of S. C. By Healy.
6. GROUP IN PLASTER, designed to ornament U. S. Capitol, but not used. By F. Pettrich.
7. UNFINISHED PORTRAIT OF GEN. ZACHARY TAYLOR, President of the U. S., born 24th Nov., 1784, died 9th July, 1850. This was commenced a few days before Gen. Taylor's death, and is the last sketch taken of him. By Vanderwort.
8. BUST OF HON. JAMES L. ORR, born 12th May, 1822. Speaker of the House of Representatives, 35th Congress.
9. GIRL FISHING. By F. Pettrich.
10. BUST OF BENJ. HALLOWELL, for many years Principal of a noted Boys' School in Alexandria, Va. By Bailey, a pupil of the school.
11. F. PETTRICH, ARTIST, AND HIS FAMILY.
12. BUST OF CLARK MILLS, the artist who designed and cast the Jackson Statue and the Washington Statue, in the city of Washington.
13. SLEEPING CHILD. Design by F. Pettrich.
14. BUST OF WM. NORRIS, the locomotive and engine builder, in Philadelphia.
15. BUST OF FRANCIS P. BLAIR, formerly editor of the "Congressional Globe." By C. Mills.
16. BUST OF CHARLES DICKENS, the celebrated novelist.
17. PORTRAIT OF CAPT. JOHN EVANS, one of the earliest American merchants. Painted by Copley.
18. A BISHOP OF ENGLAND IN OLDEN TIME. Name and artist unknown.
19. MOORISH BATTLE PIECE. Artist unknown.
20. BUST OF DANIEL WEBSTER, the illustrious statesman, born 18th January, 1782, died 24th October, 1852.
21. BUST OF MARTIN VAN BUREN, President of the U. S. Pettrich, artist.
22. BUST OF HON. JOHN C. SPENCER.
23. SLEEPING GIRL. Pettrich.
24. BUST—MISS FAIRFIELD. By C. Mills.
25. BUST—MISS HAMPTON. By C. Mills.
26. BOY HUNTER. Pettrich.
27. BUST OF DR. WM. DARLINGTON, of Westchester, Pa. One of the most noted American botanists.
28. DESIGN FOR CAPITOL.

WADE DEL.

J. RENWICK J. ARCH'T.

HOME

Insurance Company of New York

OFFICE, 112 & 114 BROADWAY.

CAPITAL STOCK, (all paid in) - - - - $1,000,000
SURPLUS, over, - - - - - - - 400,000

This Company continues to Insure Buildings, Merchandise, Ships in Port and their Cargoes, Household Furniture and Personal Property generally, against loss or damage by Fire, on favorable terms.

☞ LOSSES EQUITABLY ADJUSTED AND PROMPTLY PAID. ☜

THIS COMPANY HAS AGENTS IN ALL THE PRINCIPAL CITIES AND TOWNS IN THE UNITED STATES.

DIRECTORS:

CHARLES J. MARTIN	President.
A. F. WILLMARTH	Vice President.
WILLIAM G. LAMBERT	Firm of A. & A. Lawrence & Co.
GEORGE C. COLLINS	" Sherman, Collins & Co.
DANFORD N. BARNEY	" Wells, Fargo & Co.
LUCIUS HOPKINS	President Importers' and Traders' Bank.
THOMAS MESSENGER	Firm of T. & H. Messenger.
WILLIAM H. MELLEN	" Claflin, Mellen & Co.
CHARLES B. HATCH	" C. B. Hatch & Co.
B. WATSON BULL	" Haskell, Merrick & Bull.
HOMER MORGAN	
LEVI P. STONE	" Stone, Starr & Co.
JAMES HUMPHREY	late " Barney, Humphrey & Butler.
GEORGE PEARCE	" George Pearce & Co.
WARD A. WORK	" Ward A. Work & Son.
JAMES LOW	" James Low & Co., Louisville.
I. H. FROTHINGHAM	late " I. H. Frothingham & Co.
CHARLES A. BULKLEY	" Bulkley & Co.
CEPHAS H. NORTON	" Norton & Jewett.
ROE LOCKWOOD	" R. Lockwood & Son.
THEODORE McNAMEE	late " Bowen, McNamee & Co.
RICHARD BIGELOW	" Doan, King & Co., St. Louis.
CURTIS NOBLE	" Condit & Noble.
GEORGE D. MORGAN	" E. D. Morgan & Co.
OLIVER E. WOOD	" Willard, Wood & Co.
ALFRED S. BARNES	" A. S. Barnes & Co.
GEORGE BLISS	" Phelps, Bliss & Co.
AMOS T. DWIGHT	" Trowbridge, Dwight & Co.
LYMAN COOKE	" Cooke, Dowd, Baker & Co.
LEVI P. MORTON	" Morton, Grinnell & Co.
JOHN B. HUTCHINSON	" J. C. Howe & Co., Boston.
CHARLES P. BALDWIN	" Baldwin, Starr & Co.
JOHN G. NELSON	late " Nelson & Co.
HENRY A. HURLBUT	" Swift, Hurlbut & Co.
JESSE HOYT	" Jesse Hoyt & Co.
WM. STURGIS, JR	" Sturgis, Shaw & Co.
JOHN R. FORD	" Ford Rubber Co.
SIDNEY MASON	late " Mason & Thompson.
GEO. T. STEDMAN	" Stedman, Carlile & Shaw. Cincinnati.
CYRUS YALE, JR	" Cyrus Yale, Jr., & Co., New Orleans.
WM. R. FOSDICK	" Wm. R. & Chas. B. Fosdick.
DAVID I. BOYD	" Boyd Brothers & Co., Albany, N. Y.
F. H. COSSITT	" Cossitt, Hill & Talmadge, Memphis.
LEWIS ROBERTS	" L. Roberts & Co.
SAMUEL B. CALDWELL	" Brewer & Caldwell.

J. MILTON SMITH, *Secretary.*   CHARLES J. MARTIN, *President.*

JOHN McGEE, *Asst. Secretary.*   A. F. WILLMARTH, *Vice Pres't.*

GROVER & BAKER'S
CELEBRATED
FAMILY
Sewing Machines

The Grover and Baker Sewing Machine Co.,

HAVING GREATLY INCREASED THEIR FACILITIES FOR MANUFACTURING THEIR CELEBRATED

NOISELESS FAMILY MACHINES

WITH ALL THE RECENT IMPROVEMENTS, OFFER FOR SALE

NEW STYLES, AT REDUCED PRICES.

It is no longer questioned that these Machines are the best in use for Family Sewing. They

HEM, FELL, GATHER, AND STITCH,

In the most superior manner, and are the only machines in the market that are so well and simply made, that they may be sent into families with no other instructions than are contained in a circular which accompanies each machine, and from which

A CHILD OF TEN YEARS

May readily learn how to use them, and keep them in order.   They make upwards of

Fifteen Hundred Stitches a Minute,

And will do the sewing of a family cheaper than a seamstress can do it, even if she works at the rate of

ONE CENT AN HOUR.

Is there a husband, father, or brother in the United States, who will permit the drudgery of hand sewing in his family, when a Grover & Baker Machiue will do it better, more expeditiously, and cheaper than can possibly be done by hand?

Offices of Exhibition and Sale.—495 Broadway, New York; 18 Summer st., Boston; 730 Chestnut street, Philadelphia; 181 Baltimore street, Baltimore; 58 West Fourth street, Cincinnati; 336 Pennsylvania Avenue, Washington, D. C.

Agencies in all the principal Cities and Towns of the United States.

SEND FOR A CIRCULAR.

"My object is to call attention to the fact, that a Policy of Life Insurance is the cheapest and safest mode of making a certain provision for one's family."—BENJAMIN FRANKLIN.

"One should insure in health, as sickness may suddenly overtake the most robust, and disqualify him for insurance."

"Life Insurance the best investment. If long lived, the insured obtains a good interest on the premium paid, in cash dividends, and in most instances a very large return for a small outlay. In case of death, there is a great advantage over Savings Banks."

"The average length of human life is only thirty-three years. Of 500 persons, only one lives 80 years; and of 100, only 6 live 65 years."

NEW ENGLAND

LIFE INSURANCE COMPANY,

BOSTON, MASS. PURELY MUTUAL.

BRANCH OFFICE, 110 BROADWAY, NEW YORK CITY.

Accumulated Capital - - - - - -	$1,110,622.21
After paying Losses over - - - - -	600,000.00
And Dividends (in cash) over - - - -	500,000.00

WILLARD PHILLIPS, PRESIDENT.

DIRECTORS:

CHARLES P. CURTIS.	SEWELL TAPPAN	A. W. THAXTER, JR.
MARSHALL P. WILDER.	CHARLES HUBBARD.	GEORGE H. FOLGER.
THOS. A. DEXTER.	WILLIAM B. REYNOLDS.	PATRICK T. JACKSON.

B. F. STEVENS, SECRETARY.

The surplus is divided among *all the policy holders*, in CASH, thus affording a good and certain rate of interest upon the outlay of premiums, and avoiding the large and unnecessary accumulations of unpaid dividends of uncertain tendency, and erroneously called capital.

One-half of the first five annual premiums on life policies loaned to insurers if desired; the remaining half may be paid quarterly.

The premiums are as low as those of any reliable Company.

☞ This is the oldest American Mutual Life Insurance Company, and one of the most successful, and is purely Mutual, dividing all the Surplus Profits among all the Insured.

Insurance may be effected for the benefit of married women, beyond the reach of their husbands' creditors. Creditors may insure the lives of debtors.

Blank forms of application for Insurance, or the Company's Pamphlet, containing the charter, rules and regulations, also the annual reports, showing the condition of the Company, and information concerning Life Insurance generally, will be furnished by addressing the

BRANCH OFFICE IN NEW YORK CITY,

Metropolitan Bank Building, 110 Broadway, cor. Pine St.

JOHN HOPPER,

Agent and Attorney.

☞ THIS COMPANY HAS JUST DECLARED A DIVIDEND OF $335,763, PAYABLE (IN CASH) TO ALL HOLDING POLICIES.

I. M. SINGER & CO.'S
IMPROVED
SEWING MACHINES,
388 PENNSYLVANIA AVENUE,
(UNDER THE NATIONAL HOTEL,)
WASHINGTON CITY.

These Machines are superior for all manufacturing purposes. They are more desirable for all kinds of family sewing; capable of doing a greater variety of work; perfectly simple, easily kept in order, and are much cheaper, because they earn more money. They are just the machines for every family. We invite all to call at our Office, No. 388 Pennsylvania Avenue, and examine them and their work. The great economy in using such a machine will at once become apparent. Explanations given to all.

Circulars, illustrating all of SINGER'S SEWING MACHINES, with specimens of their work, furnished to all or sent to any address.

A good assortment of THREAD, NEEDLES, TWIST, and other machine findings kept on hand by

I. M. SINGER & CO.,
Central Office, 458 Broadway, New York.

WILLIAM H. GLOVER, AGENT,
Washington City, D. C.

SAMUEL P. HOOVER'S
WHOLESALE AND RETAIL
BOOT, SHOE, AND TRUNK
ESTABLISHMENT,
No. 320 Penna. Av., between 9th and 10th sts.,
WASHINGTON, D. C.

AT ALL TIMES ON HAND
THE LARGEST ASSORTMENT
OF

Ladies', Gentlemen's, Misses', Boys', Children's, & Servants'
BOOTS and SHOES
ALSO,

Ladies' and Gentlemen's Traveling Trunks,
VALISES, CARPET AND LEATHER BAGS, ALL QUALITIES, CHEAP FOR THE
CASH, AND CASH ONLY.

ORNAMENTAL IRON WORK!

Statuary, Fountains, Vases, Garden & House Furniture,

BEDSTEADS, BOOT-JACKS, CARD RECEIVERS, DUMB-BELLS,

FOOT-SCRAPERS, MATCH SAFES, STEP PLATES,

INKSTANDS, SPITTOONS,

LAMP POSTS, LANTERNS, COLUMNS, BRACKETS, VAULT GRATES, C

FARM GATES, UMBRELLA STANDS,

WINDOW SILLS AND CAPS,

FENCE AND HITCHING POSTS,

RAILING FOR VERANDAS, YARD FENCES, CEMETERY LOTS,

DOOR STEPS, BALCONIES, ETC.,

OF EVERY DESCRIPTION, MANUFACTURED AND FOR SALE BY

E. W. SHIPPEN,

No. 3022 Market St., West Philadelphia, Pa.

Catalogues and information furnished by W. J. RHEES, 506 H street, between 7th and 8th, Washington, D. C.

HORACE WATERS, Agent,

No. 333 BROADWAY, N. Y.,

Publisher of Music and Music Books,

DEALER IN

PIANOS, MELODEONS, ALEXANDRE ORGANS,

Organ Accordeons, Martin's celebrated and other Guitars, Violins, Tenor Viols, Violincellos, Accordeons, Flutinas, Flutes, Fifes, Clarionets, Triangles, Tuning Forks, Pipes and Hammers, Violin Bows, best Italian Strings, Brass Instruments for bands, Piano Stools and Covers, and all kinds of Musical Instruments.

SHEET MUSIC, from all the publishers in the United States; Bertini's, Huntin's, and Modern School, and all kinds of Instruction Books for the above Instruments; Church Music Books; Music elegantly bound; Music Paper, and all kinds of Music Merchandise, AT THE LOWEST PRICES.

NEW PIANOS, at $175, $200, $225, $250, and up to $800; SECOND HAND PIANOS, from $25 up to $160; NEW MELODEONS, $45, $60, $75, $100, and up to $200; SECOND HAND MELODEONS, from $30 to $80; ALEXANDRE ORGANS, with five stops, $160; nine stops, $185 and $255; thirteen stops, $250, $275, and $300; fifteen stops, $320 and $375. A liberal discount to Clergymen, Churches, Sabbath Schools, Seminaries, and Teachers. The Trade supplied at the usual trade discounts.

PIANOS, MELODEONS, AND ORGANS.

The HORACE WATERS PIANOS AND MELODEONS, for depth, purity of tone, and durability, are unsurpassed. Prices reasonable. Second Hand Pianos and Melodeons from $25 to $150.

"The Horace Waters Pianos are known as among the very best."—*Evangelist.* "We can speak of their merits from personal knowledge."—*Christian Intelligencer.* "Waters' Pianos and Melodeons challenge comparison with the finest made anywhere in the country."—*Home Journal.*

"We have two of Waters' Pianos in use in our Seminary, one of which has been severely tested for three years, and we can testify to their good quality and durability."—WOOD & GREGORY, *Mount Carroll, Ill.*

"H. WATERS, Esq.—*Dear Sir :* Having used one of your Piano-Fortes for two years past, I have found it a very *superior instrument.* ALONZO GRAY,
Principal Brooklyn Heights Seminary."

"The Piano I received from you continues to give satisfaction. I regard it as one of the best instruments in the place."—JAMES L. CLARK, *Charlestown, Va.*

"Your Piano pleases us well. It is the best one in our county."—THOMAS A. LATHAM, *Campbellton, Ga.*

The Horace Waters Pianos are built of the best and most thoroughly seasoned material. We have no doubt that buyers can do as well, perhaps better, at this than at any other house in the Union."—*Advocate and Journal.*

"Our friends will find at Mr. Waters' store the very best assortment of Music and of Pianos to be found in the United States, and we urge our southern and western friends to give him a call whenever they go to New York."—*Graham's Magazine.*

WAREROOMS, 333 BROADWAY, NEW YORK.

SABBATH SCHOOL BELL.

77,000 issued in seven months! The unprecedented sale of this book has induced the publisher to add some 36 new tunes and hymns to its present size, without extra charge, except on the cheap edition. Among the many beautiful tunes and hymns added may be found: "I ought to love my mother." "Oh, I'll be a good child, indeed I will." These, and eight others from the Bell, were sung at the Sunday-School Anniversary of the M. E. Church, at the Academy of Music, with great applause. The Bell contains nearly 200 tunes and hymns, and is one of the best collections ever issued. Price 12c; $10 per hundred, postage 2 cents; bound 20 cents; $15 per 100, postage 4 cents. Elegantly bound, embossed guilt, 25 cents; $20 per 100. *It has been introduced into many of the Public Schools.*

The BELL is published in small numbers, entitled Anniversary and Sunday School Music Books, Nos. 1, 2, 3, and 4, in order to accommodate the million. Price $2 and $3 per 100. No. 5 will soon be issued—commencement of another book. Also, Revival Music Books, Nos. 1 and 2, price $1 and $2 per 100, postage 1 cent. More than 300,000 copies of the above books have been issued the past eighteen months, and the demand is rapidly increasing. Published by

HORACE WATERS, Ag't, 333 Broadway, N. Y.

IMPORTANT TO STRANGERS!

MORRISON'S VIEWS

OF THE

PUBLIC BUILDINGS

AND

STATUES OF WASHINGTON CITY.

THIS COLLECTION CONSISTS OF

TWENTY-FIVE SUPERIOR STEEL ENGRAVINGS,

EMBRACING

EVERYTHING OF INTEREST TO A STRANGER,

With a description of the same, neatly put up in a gilt case, which can be found at any of our Bookstores.

THIS WORK NO STRANGER SHOULD BE WITHOUT.

1500 PICTORIAL ILLUSTRATIONS!!!

"GET THE BEST" WEBSTER UNABRIDGED PICTORIAL EDITION!

WEBSTER'S

UNABRIDGED

DICTIONARY.

New Pictorial Edition!

1500 Pictorial Illustrations.

We have just issued a new edition of Webster's Unabridged Dictionary, containing Fifteen Hundred Pictorial Illustrations, beautifully executed.

9,000 TO 10,000 NEW WORDS IN THE VOCABULARY, TABLE OF SYNONYMS, BY PROF. GOODRICH,

in which MORE THAN TWO THOUSAND WORDS are carefully discriminated, forming a fuller work on English Synonyms, of itself, than any other issued, besides Crabb, and believed to be in advance of that.

TABLE GIVING PRONUNCIATION OF NAMES OF 8,000 DISTINGUISHED PERSONS OF MODERN TIMES,

Peculiar use of Words and Terms in the Bible, with other new features, together with ALL THE MATTER OF PREVIOUS EDITIONS,

Comprised in a Volume of 1750 pages.

Sold by all Booksellers.

G. & C. MERRIAM,
SPRINGFIELD, MASS.

PERRY DAVIS'
VEGETABLE PAIN KILLER,
THE GREAT FAMILY MEDICINE OF THE AGE!!!

TAKEN INTERNALLY CURES	*TAKEN EXTERNALLY CURES*
SUDDEN COLDS, COUGHS, &c.,	FELONS, BOILS, AND OLD SORES,
WEAK STOMACH,	SEVERE BURNS AND SCALDS,
GENERAL DEBILITY,	CUTS, BRUISES, AND SPRAINS,
NURSING SORE MOUTH, CANKER,	SWELLING OF THE JOINTS,
LIVER COMPLAINT,	RINGWORM AND TETTER,
DYSPEPSIA OR INDIGESTION,	BROKEN BREASTS,
CRAMP AND PAIN IN THE STOMACH,	FROSTED FEET AND CHILBLAINS,
BOWEL COMPLAINT,	TOOTHACHE,
PAINTERS' COLIC, ASIATIC CHOLERA,	PAIN IN THE FACE,
DIARRHŒA AND DYSENTERY,	NEURALGIA AND RHEUMATISM.

The PAIN KILLER is by universal consent allowed to have won for itself a reputation unsurpassed in the history of medical preparations. Its instantaneous effect in the entire eradication and extinction of PAIN in all its various forms incidental to the human family, and the unsolicited written and verbal testimony of the masses in its favor, have been and are its own best advertisement.

The ingredients which enter into the PAIN KILLER, being PURELY VEGETABLE, render it a PERFECTLY SAFE and efficacious remedy taken internally, as well as for external applications, when used according to the directions. *The slight stain upon linen from its use in external applications, is readily removed by washing with a little alcohol.*

This medicine, so justly celebrated for the cure of so many of the afflictions incident to the human family, has now been before the public about EIGHTEEN YEARS, and has found its way into almost every corner of the world; and wherever it has been used, the same opinion is expressed of its real medicinal properties.

In any attack where prompt action upon the system is required, the PAIN KILLER is invaluable. Its almost instantaneous effect in RELIEVING PAIN is truly wonderful, and when used according to directions is true to its name,

A PAIN KILLER.

It is, in truth, a FAMILY MEDICINE, and should be kept in every family for immediate use. Persons traveling should always have a bottle of this remedy with them. It is not unfrequently the case that persons are attacked with disease, and before medical aid can be procured, the patient is beyond the hope of recovery. Captains of vessels should always supply themselves with a few bottles of this remedy before leaving port, as by so doing they will always be in possession of an invaluable remedy to resort to in cases of accidents and sudden attacks of sickness. It has been used in

SEVERE CASES OF THE CHOLERA

and never has failed in a single case, where it was *thoroughly applied on the first appearance of the symptoms.*

Obtain a copy of the PEOPLE'S PAMPHLET, which contains full directions for using the PAIN KILLER, together with a brief sketch of the first introduction of the medicine, recommendatory notices, certificates, &c., &c.

The present form, (adopted July 1, 1854,) in which the Pain Killer is put up, is a flat panel bottle (four sizes) with the words "DAVIS' VEGETABLE PAIN KILLER" blown in the glass, on one side of which is a miniature likeness of Perry Davis, the original inventor of the medicine; on the opposite our note of hand, to counterfeit which is held to be forgery by the laws of the United States. These labels are finely executed steel engravings, and the increased cost attending the execution and printing of the same, is incurred for the protection of the public against counterfeits, to which a less expensive style is liable.

To those who have so long used and proved the merits of our article, we would say that we shall continue to prepare our Pain Killer of the best and purest materials, and that it shall be every way worthy of their approbation as a family medicine.

PRICES, 12½ cents, 25 cents, 50 cents, and 1$ per Bottle.
BEWARE OF COUNTERFEITS AND IMITATIONS.
PERRY DAVIS & SON,
MANUFACTURERS AND PROPRIETORS, 74 HIGH ST., PROVIDENCE, R. I.

RELIGIOUS BOOK DEPOSITORY.

WM. BALLANTYNE,
498 Seventh street, two doors above Odd-Fellows' Hall,
WASHINGTON, D. C.,

Has the Depository in this city of the Publications of the American Bible Society; Methodist Book Concern; Robert Carter & Brothers; Gould & Lincoln; Presbyterian Board; American Tract Society; Evangelical Knowledge Society; American Sunday School Union; Massachusetts Sabbath School Society; and all the principal Religious Publishers. Also, a great variety of Historical and Miscellaneous Works, Hymn Books, Bibles, and Prayer Books, in plain and superb bindings; attractive and choice Juvenile Books, suitable for Gifts and Sunday School Libraries; School Books, Blank Books, Staple and Fancy Stationery; Pocket Knives, Porte-Monnaies, Portfolios, Writing Desks, Gold Pens, &c.

FIRE AND LIFE INSURANCE OFFICE
OF
J. C. LEWIS,
492 SEVENTH ST., WASHINGTON, D. C.

Life and Fire Insurance on the best terms. Capitals very large, and parties participate in the profits.

THE WHOLESALE DEPOT OF
DR. WATROUS' BALSAM,
WHICH IS CURING SO MANY OF THE AFFLICTED.

THOS. E. LLOYD.   CHAS. C. TUCKER.

TUCKER & LLOYD,
AGENTS FOR PROCURING
BOUNTY LAND AND PENSIONS,
AND DEALERS IN
LAND WARRANTS AND REAL ESTATE,
WASHINGTON, D. C.

Land Warrants bought, sold, and located. Collections made throughout the United States and Canadas. Titles to Western Lands examined, and Taxes paid for non-residents. Old Land Patents purchased, and titles to land granted for military services, and other claims for real estate, investigated and prosecuted.

Office, No. 474 Seventh st., opposite City Post Office,

O. A. DAILEY, M. D.,
DENTIST,
No. 352 Pennsylvania Avenue,
WASHINGTON, D. C.

OUR NATIONAL BUILDINGS!

W. G. METZEROTT'S
VIEWS OF WASHINGTON.

SIXTEEN BEAUTIFUL STEEL ENGRAVINGS,

Comprising all the Public Buildings and places of interest in the District.
PRICE $1. FOR SALE AT ALL BOOKSTORES.

JEROME P. CHASE,
GENERAL AGENT & CONVEYANCER,
AGENT FOR BUYING AND SELLING REAL ESTATE,

AND FOR

PROSECUTING PENSION & BOUNTY LAND CLAIMS

OFFICE:

ROOMS OF YOUNG MEN'S CHRISTIAN ASSOCIATION,

OPPOSITE BROWNS' HOTEL,

WASHINGTON, D. C.

MANUAL

OF

Public Libraries, Societies, and Institutions,

IN THE

United States and British Provinces of North America.

Historical and Statistical, with a full list of Colleges, Societies, Associations,
&c., &c., invaluable to Authors, Booksellers, Publishers, &c. One large octavo
volume of 700 pages, printed and bound in the best style. PRICE, THREE
DOLLARS.

ALSO,

GUIDE TO THE SMITHSONIAN INSTITUTION,

AND

NATIONAL MUSEUM,

With twenty-three illustrations, 8vo., 74 pages. PRICE, FIFTY CENTS.

Address   WM. J. RHEES, *Washington, D. C.*

THE
WASHINGTON MEDALLION PEN!

Merchant, Lawyer, Physician, Clergyman, Editor, Author,
Mechanic, and Farmer,

And those who are to fill these professions hereafter—School Children—you daily have occasion for writing—some much, some but little; but be it much or little, you find it a task. If you would be relieved of much of the annoyance that you now experience in writing, procure the

WASHINGTON MEDALLION PEN,
WHICH IS THE ONLY STEEL PEN MANUFACTURED IN AMERICA.

The following from the *Boston Traveler* and *Daily News* speaks of the quality distinctly enough to make further commendation unnecessary:

The Washington Medallion Pen. We wish to call the attention of our readers to this Pen. We have given it a thorough trial, and do not hesitate to recommend it as the *very best article* that we have ever held between our thumb and finger. It is as soft as a quill, and yet sufficiently firm, and it makes, when necessary, the finest hair line. It is a *satisfaction* to work with it; and if our paragraphs are ever incorrect or dull, or our spelling bad, it will not be this Pen's fault.— *Boston Traveler, Jan. 14.*

Washington Medallion Pen.— This favorite and *purely American Pen* appears to be coming into *universal use,* and is likely soon to displace the foreign article altogether. We have never used a metallic Pen of so much *delicacy* and *elasticity,* that runs so *smoothly, lasts so long,* or from which the writing fluid flows *so exactly in the right quantity,* as the Washington Medallion. *They are now used at most of the Government offices, and the sale, we are pleased to know, is enormously large and increasing.*

The following letter, the original of which we have seen, from one who well understands the use of the pen, is a high commendation.— *Daily News, Jan. 25.*

Letter from Jas. Buchanan.

Wheatland,
Tuesday, Jan. 20, 1857.

My Dear Sir: Many thanks for the box of Washington Medallion Pens. I find them better than most of the English Pens I have used, and I heartily wish the manufacturer success. The facts you state are quite interesting, and I shall retain them in my memory. I had not the most remote idea that we paid England $1,000,000 annually for steel pens.

Yours, very respectfully,
JAMES BUCHANAN.

To the Secretary
*Of the Washington Medallion,
Pen Co., 58 Cedar st., N. Y.*

These Pens have been used for more than a year in the Smithsonian Institution, and give entire satisfaction.

☞ If you have any curiosity to try these Pens, enclose two stamps to the

WASHINGTON
Medallion Pen Co.,

No. 58 CEDAR STREET,

NEW YORK.

☞ Patron's Ticket of the first series of 100,000 gross has been drawn. The number is 83,384. On presentation of the ticket bearing that number at the Office of the Company, 58 Cedar street, New York, the holder will receive One Thousand Dollars. The second series is now being issued.

THE
Metropolitan Book Store.

PHILP & SOLOMONS,

AGENTS FOR THE "METROPOLITAN MILLS."

ENGLISH, FRENCH, AND AMERICAN

STATIONERY,

OF THE

FINEST DESCRIPTION.

ENGLISH & AMERICAN PLAYING CARDS.

Foreign Books and Periodicals
IMPORTED WEEKLY.

ROUTLEDGE & CO.'S RAILWAY LIBRARY.

VISITING CARDS
ENGRAVED AND PRINTED EXPEDITIOUSLY.

PRINTING, PUBLISHING, & BOOKBINDING.

A

FINE-ART GALLERY,

FOR THE EXHIBITION OF

WORKS OF ART,

CHOICE ENGRAVINGS & CHROMO-LITHOGRAPHS
AS PUBLISHED.

NO. 332 PENNSYLVANIA AVENUE,
Between 9th and 10th Streets,
WASHINGTON CITY, D. C.

WASHINGTON:
S. E. Corner Seventh and F streets,
OPPOSITE PATENT OFFICE.

CINCINNATI:
N. E. Corner Fourth and Vine Sts.,
OPPOSITE POST OFFICE.

CONSTANT PERSONAL ATTENTION GIVEN IN U. S. PATENT OFFICE TO ALL PENDING BUSINESS.

REFER BY PERMISSION TO

Hon. JOHN McLEAN, *U. S. Supreme Court,*
Messrs. GALES A SEATON, *Washington, D. C.*

Hon. SAMUEL INGHAM, *Ex-Gov. Conn., Comm'r of Customs.*
Hon. J. H. B. LATROBE, *Baltimore, Md.*

W. D. SHEPHERD,

BOOKSELLER AND STATIONER,

CORNER OF SEVENTH AND D STREETS,

WASHINGTON, D. C.

DEALER IN PLAIN AND FANCY STATIONERY,

School and Collegiate Text Books,

DRAWING INSTRUMENTS AND ARTISTS' MATERIALS, WRITING DESKS, PORT-
FOLIOS &c., FANCY GIFT GOODS,

BIBLES, HYMNS, PSALM, AND PRAYER BOOKS,

ALL STANDARD AUTHORS, &c.   WHOLESALE AND RETAIL.

American & European Patents.

The undersigned, formerly an Examiner of Patents, and a member of the Board
of Appeals under the late Commissioner of Patents, Hon. JOSEPH HOLT, having
RESUMED the practice of his profession, attends to procuring American and European Patents.

*Inventors can also have their inventions examined prior to making an applica-
tion for a patent, by sending a pencil sketch, &c., for a fee of five dollars.*

THOMAS H. DODGE,

Counsellor at Law and Advocate in Patent Cases,
464⅞ SEVENTH STREET, WASHINGTON, D. C.

J. DENNIS, JR., SOLICITOR OF PATENTS,

PRACTICAL MACHINIST, MANUFACTURER AND DRAUGHTSMAN.

Having had twenty years' experience in building and operating machinery for manufacturing Cotton, Silk
Wool, Steam Engines, Printing Calico, &c., with ten years' experience in procuring patents, tenders his services
to inventors to make examinations of their inventions from a rough sketch or drawing and limited description,
(which may be forwarded by mail,) and compare them with the inventions in the Patent Office, and give an
opinion, whether the invention is patentable or not, for a fee of $5, and save the inventor the expense of apply-
ing for a patent, which usually costs $60, exclusive of the cost of model, and only about two-fifths of the patents
applied for are granted. His experience in making drawings, of building, and operating machinery, enables
him to understand an invention from a rough drawing and limited description, and to comprehend the points
in which the invention differs from those already patented, with the greatest facility; or for a similar fee, he
will make an examination and give an opinion as to which is the best patented machine for any purpose. He
also prepares drawings, specifications, caveats, and assignments, or procures copies from, or attends to any business connected with the Patent Office. Counsellors in patent cases can have an opinion by stating the points in
their case, and arguments prepared with the proper authorities cited to sustain the same, with depositions if
necessary. He will also attend as Counsellor or Advocate in patent causes in any Court. N. B.—All communications considered strictly confidential. Rejected applications carefully examined for $5. Appeals from the de-
cisions of the Commissioner of Patents taken to one of the Judges of the Circuit Court for a moderate fee. Circulars containing important information for Inventors and Patentees forwarded to any person desiring them.
Office, 371 F st. north, opposite the south front of the Patent Office, near 9th st., Washington, D. C

FOR LIBRARIANS, AUTHORS, BOOKSELLERS, PUBLISHERS, ETC.

JUST PUBLISHED,

MANUAL OF LIBRARIES,

Societies and Institutions,

IN THE

THE UNITED STATES AND BRITISH PROVINCES OF NORTH AMERICA,

BY

WILLIAM J. RHEES, CHIEF CLERK OF THE SMITHSONIAN INSTITUTION.

IT CONTAINS AN HISTORICAL AND STATISTICAL ACCOUNT, WITH A FULL LIST, OF LIBRARIES,
  COLLEGES AND COLLEGE SOCIETIES,
    ACADEMIES, SEMINARIES, AND HIGH SCHOOLS,
      INSTITUTIONS FOR THE DEAF, DUMB, BLIND, INSANE,
        AGRICULTURAL, HISTORICAL, SCIENTIFIC, MERCANTILE,
          YOUNG MEN'S CHRISTIAN, AND OTHER ASSOCIATIONS.

Indicating those Libraries which have received sets of the United States Government public documents, &c.

This List is invaluable to all who have circulars, pamphlets, reports, &c., to distribute.

This volume contains articles on the construction, lighting, heating, and ventilating of Library Buildings; the arrangement, classification, and catalogues of books: salaries of librarians; number of volumes in different languages in public libraries; number and kind of books most read; statistical tables, and in fact every species of information which could be collected relative to public libraries and institutions.

It is the result of several years' labor, and the examination of all the material collected by the

Smithsonian Institution and Government Departments at Washington.

IT ALSO CONTAINS ACCOUNTS OF

COMMON SCHOOL LIBRARIES,

WITH THE LATEST STATISTICS;

SUNDAY SCHOOL, MILITARY, AND OTHER LIBRARIES.

☞ The whole forms a large octavo volume of 700 pages, printed and bound in the best style.

Price Three Dollars per Copy.

PUBLISHED FOR THE AUTHOR BY J. B. LIPPINCOTT & CO., PHILADELPHIA.

☞ For copies address the Publishers, or

W. J. RHEES, WASHINGTON, D. C.

REMOVED FROM NO. 422 BROADWAY,

JAMES GREEN,

IMPORTER AND MANUFACTURER OF

PHILOSOPHICAL INSTRUMENTS

AND

Chemical Apparatus,

173 & 175 GRAND ST., bet. BROADWAY and BOWERY,

NEW YORK CITY.

MAKER OF METEOROLOGICAL INSTRUMENTS
TO THE SMITHSONIAN INSTITUTION.

EVERY VARIETY OF

Optical, Mathematical, and Philosophical Instruments

ON HAND, AS

MECHANICAL POWERS,
HYDROSTATIC APPARATUS,
AIR PUMPS OF ALL SIZES,
ELECTRICAL MACHINES AND APPARATUS,
GALVANIC BATTERIES,
ELECTRO-MAGNETIC APPARATUS,

ASTRONOMICAL AND OTHER DIAGRAMS, in great
 variety.
MAGIC LANTERNS,
ACHROMATIC AND OTHER MICROSCOPES,
SURVEYING COMPASSES,
DRAWING INSTRUMENTS.

A PARTICULAR DESCRIPTION OF

GREEN'S STANDARD BAROMETER,

WITH

Thermometers, and other Meteorological Instruments,

Adopted by and made under the direction of the Smithsonian Institution, is given in the
Annual Report of the Institution for 1855, by Prof. Henry, and will be furnished gratuitously,
together with meteorological blanks, &c., on application to the Smithsonian Institution.

PRICE LISTS FURNISHED ON APPLICATION.
DESCRIPTIONS AND INSTRUCTIONS FOR USE ARE SENT WITH THE INSTRU-
MENTS.

THREE CENTURIES
OF
SCIENCE IN AMERICA

An Arno Press Collection

Adams, John Quincy. **Report of the Secretary of State upon Weights and Measures.** 1821.

Archibald, Raymond Clare. **A Semicentennial History of the American Mathematical Society: 1888-1938** *and* **Semicentennial Addresses of the American Mathematical Society.** 2 vols. 1938.

Bond, William Cranch. **History and Description of the Astronomical Observatory of Harvard College** *and* **Results of Astronomical Observations Made at the Observatory of Harvard College.** 1856.

Bowditch, Henry Pickering. **The Life and Writings of Henry Pickering Bowditch.** 2 vols. 1980.

Bridgman, Percy Williams. **The Logic of Modern Physics.** 1927.

Bridgman, Percy Williams. **Philosophical Writings of Percy Williams Bridgman.** 1980.

Bridgman, Percy Williams. **Reflections of a Physicist.** 1955.

Bush, Vannevar. **Science the Endless Frontier.** 1955.

Cajori, Florian. **The Chequered Career of Ferdinand Rudolph Hassler.** 1929.

Cohen, I. Bernard, editor. **The Career of William Beaumont and the Reception of His Discovery.** 1980.

Cohen, I. Bernard, editor. **Benjamin Peirce: "Father of Pure Mathematics" in America.** 1980.

Cohen, I. Bernard, editor. **Aspects of Astronomy in America in the Nineteenth Century.** 1980.

Cohen, I. Bernard, editor. **Cotton Mather and American Science and Medicine: With Studies and Documents Concerning the Introduction of Inoculation or Variolation.** 2 vols. 1980.

Cohen, I. Bernard, editor. **The Life and Scientific Work of Othniel Charles Marsh.** 1980.

Cohen, I. Bernard, editor. **The Life and the Scientific and Medical Career of Benjamin Waterhouse: With Some Account of the Introduction of Vaccination in America.** 2 vols. 1980.

Cohen, I. Bernard, editor. **Research and Technology.** 1980.

Cohen, I. Bernard, editor. **Thomas Jefferson and the Sciences.** 1980.

Cooper, Thomas. **Introductory Lecture** *and* **A Discourse on the Connexion Between Chemistry and Medicine.** 2 vols. in one. 1812/1818.

Dalton, John Call. **John Call Dalton on Experimental Method.** 1980.

Darton, Nelson Horatio. **Catalogue and Index of Contributions to North American Geology: 1732-1891.** 1896.

Donnan, F[rederick] G[eorge] and Arthur Haas, editors. **A Commentary on the Scientific Writings of J. Willard Gibbs** *and* Duhem, Pierre. **Josiah-Willard Gibbs: A Propos de la Publication de ses Mémoires Scientifiques.** 3 vols. in two. 1936/1908.

Dupree, A[nderson] Hunter. **Science in the Federal Government: A History of Policies and Activities to 1940.** 1957.

Ellicott, Andrew. **The Journal of Andrew Ellicott.** 1803.

Fulton, John F. **Harvey Cushing: A Biography.** 1946.

Getman, Frederick H. **The Life of Ira Remsen.** 1940.

Goode, George Brown. **The Smithsonian Institution 1846-1896: The History of its First Half Century.** 1897.

Hale, George Ellery. **National Academies and the Progress of Research.** 1915.

Harding, T. Swann. **Two Blades of Grass: A History of Scientific Development in the U.S. Department of Agriculture.** 1947.

Hindle, Brooke. **David Rittenhouse.** 1964.

Hindle, Brooke, editor. **The Scientific Writings of David Rittenhouse.** 1980.

Holden, Edward S[ingleton]. **Memorials of William Cranch Bond, Director of the Harvard College Observatory, 1840-1859, and of his Son, George Phillips Bond, Director of the Harvard College Observatory, 1859-1865.** 1897.

Howard, L[eland] O[sslan]. **Fighting the Insects: The Story of an Entomologist, Telling the Life and Experiences of the Writer.** 1933.

Jaffe, Bernard. **Men of Science in America.** 1958.

Karpinski, Louis C. **Bibliography of Mathematical Works Printed in America through 1850.** Reprinted with Supplement and Second Supplement. 1940/1945.

Loomis, Elias. **The Recent Progress of Astronomy: Especially in the United States.** 1851.

Merrill, Elmer D. **Index Rafinesquianus: The Plant Names Published by C.S. Rafinesque with Reductions, and a Consideration of his Methods, Objectives, and Attainments.** 1949.

Millikan, Robert A[ndrews]. **The Autobiography of Robert A. Millikan.** 1950.

Mitchel, O[rmsby] M[acKnight]. **The Planetary and Stellar Worlds: A Popular Exposition of the Great Discoveries and Theories of Modern Astronomy.** 1848.

Organisation for Economic Co-operation and Development. **Reviews of National Science Policy: United States.** 1968.

Packard, Alpheus S. **Lamarck: The Founder of Evolution; His Life and Work.** 1901.

Pupin, Michael. **From Immigrant to Inventor.** 1930.

Rhees, William J. **An Account of the Smithsonian Institution.** 1859.

Rhees, William J. **The Smithsonian Institution: Documents Relative to its History.** 2 vols. 1901.

Rhees, William J. **William J. Rhees on James Smithson.** 2 vols. in one. 1980.

Scott, William Berryman. **Some Memories of a Palaeontologist.** 1939.

Shryock, Richard H. **American Medical Research Past and Present.** 1947.

Shute, Michael, editor. **The Scientific Work of John Winthrop.** 1980.

Silliman, Benjamin. **A Journal of Travels in England, Holland, and Scotland, and of Two Passages over the Atlantic in the Years 1805 and 1806.** 2 vols. 1812.

Silliman, Benjamin. **A Visit to Europe in 1851.** 2 vols. 1856

Silliman, Benjamin, Jr. **First Principles of Chemistry.** 1864.

Smith, David Eugene and Jekuthiel Ginsburg. **A History of Mathematics in America before 1900.** 1934.

Smith, Edgar Fahs. **James Cutbush: An American Chemist.** 1919.

Smith, Edgar Fahs. **James Woodhouse: A Pioneer in Chemistry, 1770-1809.** 1918.

Smith, Edgar Fahs. **The Life of Robert Hare: An American Chemist (1781-1858).** 1917.

Smith, Edgar Fahs. **Priestley in America: 1794-1804.** 1920.

Sopka, Katherine. **Quantum Physics in America: 1920-1935** (Doctoral Dissertation, Harvard University, 1976). 1980.

Steelman, John R[ay]. **Science and Public Policy: A Report to the President.** 1947.

Stewart, Irvin. **Organizing Scientific Research for War: The Administrative History of the Office of Scientifc Research and Development.** 1948.

Stigler, Stephen M., editor. **American Contributions to Mathematical Statistics in the Nineteenth Century.** 2 vols. 1980.

Trowbridge, John. **What is Electricity?** 1899.

True. Alfred. **Alfred True on Agricultural Experimentation and Research.** 1980.

True, F[rederick] W., editor. **The Semi-Centennial Anniversary of the National Academy of Sciences: 1863-1913** *and* **A History of the First Half-Century of the National Academy of Sciences: 1863-1913.** 2 vols. 1913.

Tyndall, John. **Lectures on Light: Delivered in the United States in 1872-73.** 1873.

U.S. House of Representatives. **Annual Report of the Board of Regents of the Smithsonian Institution...A Memorial of George Brown Goode together with a selection of his Papers on Museums and on the History of Science in America.** 1901.

U.S. National Resources Committee. **Research: A National Resource.** 3 vols. in one. 1938-1941.

U.S. Senate. **Testimony Before the Joint Commission to Consider the Present Organizations of the Signal Service, Geological Survey, Coast and Geodetic Survey, and the Hydrographic Office of the Navy Department.** 2 vols. 1866.